RHODES

LINDOS - KAMIROS - FILERIMOS

ISBN 960-213-007-5

Copyright 1982, 1984

by

EKDOTIKE ATHENON S.A.

1, Vissarionos Street

Athens 106 72, Greece

PRINTED AND BOUND IN GREECE

by

EKDOTIKE HELLADOS S.A.

An affiliated company

8, Philadelphias Street, Athens

Publishers: George A. Christopoulos, John C. Bastias

Translation: David Hardy

Editor of original edition: I. Douskou

Editor of present edition: E. Karpodini-Dimitriadi

Art Director of original edition: A. Simou

Layout of present edition: P. Pavlidou

Covers: A. Simou

Special Photography: M. Skiadaressis, Y. Skouroyannis,

A. Spyropoulos, S. Tsavdaroglou

RHODES

LINDOS - KAMIROS - FILERIMOS

The Palace of the Grand Masters and the Museum

A.B. TATAKI

Archaeologist

EKDOTIKE ATHENON S.A.
Athens 1997

Preface by Professor Manolis Andronicos

Every corner of Greece has an age-long history, which is attested by the monuments standing as tangible witnesses to it. It would be no exaggeration, however, to claim for Rhodes a special position in the whole of the Greek world. A frontier island on the southeastern periphery of the Greek sea, it formed a connection between the Greek world proper and Asia Minor, and ensured contact with Cyprus and the coasts of Syria and Palestine beyond. The geographical position and physical terrain of the island were favourable to its historical development and made a decisive contribution to determining its fortunes throughout the centuries.

The Greek myths evidence the fascination that the sun-drenched island exercised on the imagination of the Greeks. When Zeus divided up the world, we are told, he forgot Helios (the Sun), who was not present. On his return, the latter complained of the injustice, and the "father of gods and men" expressed his preparedness to begin again and make a new allocation. Helios did not allow this, however, for he had seen emerging from the foaming sea, a rich island that had hitherto lain hidden beneath the surface of the ocean, and he chose this as his allotted portion. There he lay with Rhodos and fathered seven children, through whom he became grandfather of Kamiros, Lindos and Ialysos; these three divided the beautiful island between them, and gave their names to the three famous cities of ancient Rhodes.

The modern visitor quickly becomes aware that the god has not ceased to love his ancient land, which he bathes continuously in the light and heat of his rays. The visitor who enjoys the sun and sea of the island, however, may also become acquainted with its history, if he has a guide to accompany him amongst the remains of the monuments resulting from the creative activity of the Rhodians throughout their long and fluctuating history. In the island as a whole, and particularly within the city itself, there are monuments ranging from the creations of the Mycenaean period, which may be seen in the Museum, to the modern buildings that spread out both inside and outside the city. The visitor frequently comes upon unexpected monuments in a surprisingly good state of preservation. The medieval walled city, the Kastro, enclosed within the walls, with its Gothic buildings, is unique. The presence of these exotic buildings on a Greek island adds to their fascination, but the visitor should not confine himself within the limits of the medieval city, for if he does, he will deprive himself of the picture of Greek Rhodes which, though perhaps less impressive, is nonetheless more authentic. Kamiros, with the ruins of its ancient Greek city; Ialysos, with its fine 4th-century B.C. monumental fountain; and above all Lindos, with its imposing acropolis and the temple of Athena Lindia; all these sites offer an excellent comprehensive picture of this outer bastion of the ancient Greek world.

The following pages are designed to help the visitor by supplementing his personal experience with useful information, without offering numerous unnecessary opinions to cloud the impression of the island that each individual forms with own eyes.

THE HISTORY OF THE ISLAND

Introduction

Rhodes is the largest island in the Dodecanese. This name, meaning twelve islands, is now generally used to designate the complex of islands in the SE Aegean which in fact number 13 or 14, and which are also called the Southern Sporades. (The other islands are: Astypalaia, Chalke, Karpathos, Kasos, Telos, Nisyros, Kalymnos, Leros, Patmos, Syme, Kos, Kastellorizo, Leipsoi).

Rhodes has a total area of 1412 square kms., with a maximum length of 78 kms (SW-NE) and a maximum width of 38 kms. The terrain is mountainous for the most part and the plains are limited in extent, though not so much as on most Aegean islands. They are to be found near the coast, but are not the only cultivable areas; a large number of small plateaux and the foothills of the mountains are also cultivated. The highest mountain is Atavyros (1215 m. a.s.l.), which lies to the west of the Atavyros range, of which it is the continuation, while the thickly wooded Profitis Ilias (798 m. a.s.l.) rises in the east. All the remaining mountains are much lower and are scarcely high enough to merit the term; the imposing Filerimos, for example, is a mere 270 m. high. The physical terrain of the island exhibits great variety; there are a good number of winter torrents (over 10), most of which flow into the sea on the east coast. The coasts of Rhodes alternate between the gentle shores that make up most of the east coast and sheer rocky promontories and headlands. The cape of Ammouthia, also known as Koubournou, is on the NE edge of the city of Rhodes and there are extensive sandy beaches and fine bathing on both sides of it. On the east coast is the impressive promontory on which Lindos stands, surrounded by small harbours and anchorages. The west coast has the distinctive rocky mass of the Monolithos, while in the south there is Prasonisi, which appears to be an island when the sea rises and covers the narrow strip of land connecting

◄ *1. Part of the sanctuary of Athena at Lindos.*

2. Rhodes, the flower of the Dodecanese (Rhodon is the ancient Greek for rose), has been one of the major tourist centres in the Mediterranean for many years. There are many factors to account for its attraction; emerald-green coasts with their changing moods, sometimes peaceful and sometimes stormy, luxuriant foliage, outstanding monuments of ancient, Byzantine and medieval Greece, and a mild climate. Inevitably, tourism has discovered the great charm of the island, and nowadays Rhodes is a modern tower of Babel during the summer months. The entrance to Mandraki, the small harbour in which the pleasure boats are usually moored.

3. The harbour of Rhodes, from the palace of the Grand Master.

4. *Over and above the wealth of beauty bestowed by nature, the days of Rhodes' former glory have also set their seal on the island. Time and men have conspired to destroy the temples and castles, but there are enough remains to make Rhodes a perfect place to become acquainted with the past. General view of the fortified acropolis and the village at Lindos.*

5-6. *Two of the most famous beaches of Rhodes, one in the city and the other just outside it.*

4

it with the mainland. There are some islands proper near Rhodes, Halimnia and a series of smaller ones that are really just rocks – Makri, Strongyli, Chtenia etc. – in the west, and Pentanisos and Tetrapolis on the east coast opposite Lindos.

Two of the island's harbours, in the city of Rhodes, are in use at present: the commercial harbour which handles passenger and cargo ships and that at Mandraki for small vessels.

The morphological variety of the island, which is typical also of the Aegean, is the product of the disturbed geological past of the area. Echoes of this past are preserved in the aetiological myth that the island rose up out of the sea, and also in the unending series of earthquakes that have afflicted the island during the last 300 years and have made a deep mark on its historical development. Geographically Rhodes is situated on the borders between the two worlds – East and West. This circumstance ensured it a troubled history, thanks to its great potential as the commercial crossroads of three continents – Europe, Asia and Africa (through Egypt); at the same time, however, it made a basic contribution to the long periods of prosperity enjoyed throughout its history. The island, moreover, has a mild climate and is rich in vegetation, thanks to the exceptionally high number of hours of sunshine it receives and to its humidity, which is considerably higher than the average for the other Aegean islands. As a result, Rhodes is a particularly pleasant place to reside and the reward for the farmer's toils is relatively good. The few rains that fall, mainly during the winter months, do not detract from the agreeable climate and the summer heat is tempered by a refreshing, often strong, breeze.

The population of Rhodes is 87,945 according to the 1981 census. The largest increase in population is that of the city of Rhodes, which had 41,425 inhabitants in 1981; the real figure must be higher since many of the inhabitants are still enrolled in the villages or the islands in which they were born. The rest of the population is distributed between 43 "Communities", most of which are in the plains and the largest of which is the village of Ialysos (fomerly Trianda). In recent years there has been a large movement of the population to the city of Rhodes, the most important urban center in the island and the Prefecture. Many of the factors contributing to the emergence of this phenomenon are common to the rest of Greece, but account should taken of the enormous development of tourism, which has transformed the economy of the island in recent years. The tourist movement, moreover, which is continually increasing, is producing changes in the social as well as the economic life of the island. Part of the population, however, is still engaged in agriculture and stock-breeding.

7-9. Rhodes reached great heights of cultural, as well as political and economic development in Archaic times, as is reflected in the richness of the works of art from that period. Above: plaques of electrum representing the Mistress of Animals. Below: delicately worked electrum pendants found at Kamiros. Paris, Louvre.

9

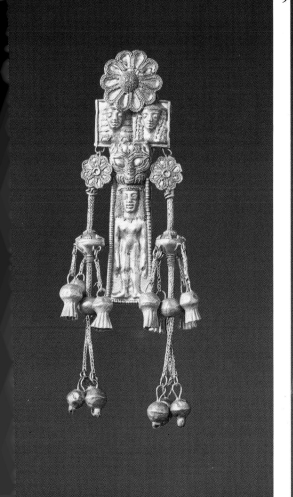

The cultivable area of the island forms about 18% of the whole, and the main products are wine, oil, tobacco, garden produce, cereals and tree-crops. Cattle-raising yields good results, since 34% of the terrain is pasture land. In addition to goats, sheep and cows, birds have begun to be raised on a systematic basis in recent years.

The island's forests are also a source of revenue; they cover 37% its territory, and though this is a small proportion in comparison with the percentage of mountainous area, it is quite large when compared with the total forested area of Greece. The over-exploitation of the forests during the Turkish period led to their disappearance in some areas, which have remained bare, such as Mount Atavyros. Profitis Ilias is richly wooded, mainly with pine, though there is also a large number of varieties of cypress, plane, oak etc. In the NW of the island there is a green valley with plane trees and laurels, which has a myriad butterflies, a delightful feature and a great tourist attraction. The forests of Rhodes are the home of a species of deer called *platoni,* which is very rare in Greece. The animal is one of the island's emblems and it is illegal to hunt it. The pines and the thyme, along with the hosts of flowers make for the production of good quality honey.

The trade of Rhodes increased significantly as a result of the tariff concessions granted to the Dodecanese when it was incorporated into the Greek state and with the facilitation of direct imports from abroad.

Rhodes in Mythological Tradition

The island possessed all the features necessary to stimulate the fertile imagination of its people. Memories of geological events; its natural beauty; successive waves of settlers and the assimilation of diverse racial groups during the prehistoric period; contact at an early point in time with the larger world, mainly of the East – all these factors combined to produce a series of captivating myths. These represent a dim memory of actual events, or a later reconstruction of events that occurred in the more or less distant past. A glance at them will give some idea of the fertile mind of the period and of the men who invented these charming or fearful stories.

Helios (the Sun), the god to whom the island belonged, was one of the most important heroes of the myths connected with Rhodes. According to the VII Olympic Ode by Pindar, in praise of Diagoras, the Rhodian Olympic victor, Helios was absent on his daily journey round the earth when the gods were dividing up the world between them, and they forgot to allot him a share. Zeus did not wish to wrong him, and was preparing to make a new distribution when Helios returned. The latter did not allow this, however, for he had already made his choice: he had seen Rhodes rise from the sea in which it had been submerged. According to myth, Rhodos, or Rhode, was a Nymph, the daughter of Poseidon and Halia, a sister of the Telchines, who were the island's first inhabitants. Another version records that Rhodos was the daughter of Amphitrite, and a third the daughter of Aphrodite. The myth first mentioned claims that Helios had seven sons and one daughter by Rhodos, and that one of them in turn had three sons, Kamiros, Ialysos and Lindos, who divided the island into three parts, so that each of them had his own city.

The original inhabitants of the island, the Telchines, were a strange race with monstrous physical characteristics and great skill in the arts, though they combined these with trickery and sorcery. They lived on Rhodes before it was sunk, but fled in various directions on being informed of the impending flood by Zeus. Their sister, the Nymph loved by Helios, was the sole inheritor of the island. The children of Helios and Rhodos were called the Heliades, which is one of the names in mythology for the earliest inhabitants of the island.

In many of the myths Rhodes is connected with Crete – a reflection of the Minoan settlement of the island. One of these is the myth of Althaimenes, grandson of Minos. In order to escape the oracle that prophesied he would kill his father Katreus, Althaimenes left Crete with a number of companions and came to Rhodes, arriving near Kamiros at a site which he called Kretenia in memory of his fatherland. Here he settled and won the respect of the inhabitants of the region. He built a temple to Zeus Atavyrios, above Kamiros; on a clear day, he could see his fatherland in the distance from Atavyros. In the end, however, just as in the similar myth of Oedipus, the hero did kill his father, for when Katreus came to Rhodes in search of his son many years later, Althaimenes failed to recognise him and took him for a pirate. When he discovered that the oracle had been fulfilled, despite his long self-imposed exile, he called on the earth to open and swallow him up. The Rhodians subsequently honoured Althaimenes as a hero.

Danaos called at Lindos on his way to Greece. He was fleeing from Libya, where he had been king, with his 50 daughters, the Danaids, to save them from their brother who was going to kill them, according to an oracle. Danaos built a temple to Athena and erected a statue of her in gratitude for the assistance she had given him during the journey. Three of the Danaids died on the island and, according to this tradition, it was from them that the three cities of Rhodes received their names.

Kadmos of Phoenicia also visited Rhodes during his wanderings in search of Europa. He built a temple of Poseidon there and left some of his followers behind to take care of it. He also dedicated a bronze cauldron to Athena Lindia, which bore an inscription in the Phoenician script; the introduction of the Phoenician alphabet to Greece thus began in Rhodes, according to this myth.

Tlepolemos, the son of Herakles, did not leave Greece along with the other Herakleidae, but stayed behind in the Peloponnese and settled at Argos, where he accidentally killed Likymnios, his father's uncle. The other Herakleidae threatened to kill him, and Tlepolemos, after consulting the oracle of Apollo, constructed ships, which he manned with many of his companions. After many hardships and wanderings, he arrived at Rhodes, where he settled. According to the *Iliad,* Tlepolemos was the first Achaean to colonise Rhodes, and also the founder of the three cities. He took part in the expedition against Troy with a contingent of nine ships, and confronted the

Lycian leader Sarpedon in a duel which resulted in his death. The myth reflects events of the Mycenaean age, when the Achaeans were making numerous efforts to win territory on the Asia Minor coast opposite. The Rhodians honoured Tlepolemos as their founder (*oikistes*) and celebrated a festival in his honour, the *Tlepolemeia*. His wife Polyxo ruled the island after his death. One version of the fate of the fair Helen claims that after the capture of Troy she was pursued to Rhodes where Polyxo had her captured and hanged, in revenge for the death of her husband in the war fought on Helen's account. Afterwards she had a shrine on Rhodes, where she was worshipped as *Helen Dendritis* (after the tree from which she was hanged).

Prehistoric Period

Until recently no installation dating from the Neolithic period or the Early Bronze Age had been located on Rhodes, although the neighbouring islands – Kos, Kalymnos – and those further afield – Lesbos, Chios, Samos and Cyprus – have produced considerable evidence from these periods. Recent investigations in two caves on Rhodes, one on Mount Koumelos, near the village of Archangelos in the east part of the island, and the other at Kalythies, close to the city of Rhodes, have brought to light sherds and stone vessels of Neolithic and Early Bronze Age date. These, together with random pre-Mycenaean finds from other locations, indicate that the island was inhabited from very early times. Rhodes is situated close to the Asia Minor coast and to the islands that bridge the gap between Mainland Greece and Crete (which were already flourishing during these periods), making communication beween the two not only desirable but also feasible, even with primitive means of sea travel. The existence of pre-Hellenic tribes on Rhodes, as in the areas of Mainland Greece and Asia Minor, is attested by linguistic evidence. The place names Kamiros, Lindos, Ialysos, Atavyris or Atavyrion, and possibly also the name of the island itself, were given to these sites by the earliest inhabitants, who were related to the peoples of Asia Minor, the other islands and Mainland Greece.

The expansionist economic policy of Minoan Crete in the middle of the 2nd millennium B.C. has been detected on Rhodes in the establishment of a trading post at the site of Trianda (Ialysos) in the NE part of the island. The earliest Mycenaean settlements made their appearance shortly afterwards, and Minoan Ialysos was abandoned. The Mycenaean settlements quickly doubled in number and occupied the whole of the northern part of the island. Achaeans from the Argolid settled on Rhodes, following in the path of their goods, which had already conquered the markets of the East. The extensive cemeteries in the region of Kamiros and at Ialysos furnish evidence for this period. The retention in historical times of the name Achaea for the acropolis of Ialysos demonstrates the extent and importance of the Mycenaean settlement. The place name *Ahhijawa* occurs in the Hittite archives of this period: this has been identified with Mycenaean Achaea, but the attempt to associate it with Rhodes of the Mycenaean period has not met with general acceptance. In the 12th century B.C. the E. Mediterranean was in a state of turmoil, usually attributed to the invasion of the *Sea Peoples*. As a result of this there was a new movement of Achaeans to the areas familiar to them in the East and an increase in the number of their settlements on Rhodes. The end of the Mycenaean world coincided with the appearance of new Hellenic tribes, the Dorians, who established themselves in areas which had previously enjoyed prosperity, to a greater or lesser degree. The Dorians who migrated to Rhodes came from the region of Argos. In Rhodes, as in the rest of Greece, the fusion of the various cultural elements in the years that followed gave birth to the civilisation whose renown was to live forever.

Classical and Hellenistic Periods

The Period of the Island's Prosperity

The Dorians who colonised the SE Aegean were divided into autonomous Dorian states, of which three were on Rhodes (Lindos, Kamiros and Ialysos), one on Kos and two on the Karian coast (Knidos and Halikarnassos). These states formed the *Dorian hexapolis,* with its centre at the sanctuary of Triopian Apollo in Knidos, at the same period that the Ionians organised the *Panionion* (700 B.C.). The Rhodian states had already for some time possessed all the Dorian features, namely the Dorian dialect and political organisation, the division into three tribes, the cults and customs, while at the same time they displayed a tendency towards autonomy. Their economic development was swift, and from the 8th century B.C. onwards they began to take part in a network of commercial exchanges between the East, Attica and Crete. From the East they learnt once more how to work the precious materials in which their Achaean ancestors had shown such skill. The art of writing, which had been forgotten for some centuries, reappeared in a new form after the development of commercial relations with the Phoenicians in the second half of the 8th century B.C. Some of the earliest Greek inscriptions have been found on Rhodes.

In the following century Rhodes competed with Corinth for the markets of the West. At the same time Corinthian pottery conquered the Rhodian market. The Rhodians held first place amongst the Greeks trading in Syria, Cyprus and the ports of the eastern Mediterranean. At the beginning of the 7th century B.C. inhabitants from Lindos founded two colonies: one in the West, Gela, on the SW coast of Sicily, which also received colonists from Crete, and the other in the East, Phaselis, on the coast of Pamphylia. It was during this same century that Rhodes' relations with Egypt began — relations desired by Rhodes because the island had a chronic insufficiency of cereals. The Rhodians had a good position in Naukratis, the Greek trading post on the Nile Delta. Their commercial interests also took them to the west of the Mediterranean, where they founded colonies as far afield as the Balearic Isles and Spain.

The island's economic prosperity is also clear from the numismatic evidence. Kamiros struck coins in the 6th century B.C. while Lindos and Ialysos began to mint their own coinages from the 5th century B.C. Kleoboulos of Lindos lived about 600 B.C. As tyrant of the city he ruled it wisely for 40 years, fostering its development. He was a contemporary of Solon, and like him was included in the list of the Seven Sages of Ancient Greece.

The Rhodians offered resistance to the Persian forces sent by Darius in 491/90 B.C. to subjugate Greece. Datis, the commander of the Persian army, laid siege to Lindos, but broke it off on learning that the goddess Athena had worked a miracle and supplied the water that was needed by the besieged. In the following Persian campaign, however, the Rhodians were compelled to fight with their ships on the Persian side at Salamis. After the end of the Persian Wars, the three cities on Rhodes became members of the 1st Athenian Confederacy (478/77 B.C.) and paid tribute.

In the Peloponnesian War (431-404 B.C.) the Rhodians took the part of the Athenians against the Spartans and the other Peloponnesians, with whom they were related ethnically. They revolted from the Confederacy in 412 B.C., after fighting on the Athenian side in the disastrous Sicilian expedition.

It was at this point that negotiations must have begun between the three cities with a view to the organisation of a new state. The synoecism of the three ancient cities took place in 408 B.C., and was an event of great significance in the history, not only of the islands but also of the Mediterranean. No ancient historian explains the reasons behind this decision. Some of them are self-evident: it would be easier to meet external threats, and the site of the new city was greatly superior to the other three. The city of Rhodes possessed five harbours, three of which were excellent, and this was a fundamental factor in its future development. The official name of the newly organised state was *Damos Rhodion* (city of Rhodians). The demes in the old cities continued to exist and still had local councils, the *mastroi,* to deal with internal affairs. The new city had an assembly *(ekklesia),* a council *(boule),* which changed every six months, and five *prytaneis,* who changed with the council and who were the state's executive authority. The *eponymous archon,* who gave his name to the year, was the priest of Helios.

The 4th century B.C. saw the new state wavering between the two powers, Sparta and Athens. Rhodes joined the 2nd Athenian Confederacy when it was founded in 377 B.C. Shortly afterwards, however (363 B.C.), it entered into alliance with Thebes, which was turning against Athens. This was followed by the war in which Athens clashed with her allies, and with Rhodes, and which resulted in the dissolution of the Confederacy. In the middle of the century the existence of Rhodes as an independent state was seriously threatened when Mausolos, the ruler of Karia, succeeded in governing it by establishing an oligarchy that acted as his instrument (355/54 B.C.). Subsequently, Artemisia, successor to Mau-

10-11. The coins issued by the city of Rhodes had its emblem, the rhodon *on one side, and the head of the sun god, Helios, on the other. Athens, Numismatic Museum.*

10

11

solos, captured Rhodes by treachery and killed her most important opponents (351 B.C.). The Rhodians appealed to Athens for help, and Demosthenes delivered his speech "In defence of Rhodian freedom", but to no effect. It was only after several years that the Rhodians succeeded in throwing off the Karian yoke.

It was at this period that the Kingdom of Macedonia appeared on the scene in Greek history. The Rhodians aligned themselves with Alexander the Great and received a Macedonian garrison in their city. They also sent ships to assist Alexander in his siege of Tyre. The founding of Alexandria in 331 B.C. was of great importance in the history of Rhodes, for it gave greater impetus to the island's economic relations with Egypt. Rhodes seems to have served as the model for the political organisation of Alexandria, and a small island off the harbour was called *Antirrhodos* (Rival to Rhodes). The Macedonian garrison was driven out of Rhodes after the death of Alexander.

The power of the island had increased during the 4th century B.C.; its main export, wine, had advanced from the N. coast of the Black Sea to the "barbarian" markets of the Scythians, Maiotians and Sindians, while Rhodes itself appears, before the synoecism, to have secured possessions on the Asia Minor coast opposite the island.

In the troubled period that followed the death of Alexander the Great, Rhodes was unable to maintain for long the neutrality she desired. Antigonos and his son Demetrios wanted the island to take part in their war against Ptolemy of Egypt. Its refusal compelled Demetrios to turn against it in order to secure freedom of movement in the war against Egypt. The siege of Rhodes by Demetrios (305/4 B.C.) is one of the most famous in the ancient world, because of the huge size of the besieging force and the modern technical equipment used in the attempt to capture the city. When Demetrios came to Rhodes he was already known as "The Besieger", a title he had acquired as a result of his success at Salamis in Cyprus. The siege of Rhodes, however, which lasted for a whole year, failed to justify his reputation; the city emerged intact, largely thanks to the valour of its heroic inhabitants. The Rhodians sold the siege machines left behind by Demetrios and used the enormous revenue from them (300 talants) to set up the statue of Helios – the *Colossus of Rhodes.*

With the end of the siege by Demetrios, there began a period, lasting roughly 150 years, during which Rhodes reached the highest point of economic prosperity and political renown. Rhodes played a role of prime importance in Greek affairs during this troubled epoch, which was marked by continual clashes between the powers that succeeded to the short-lived empire of Alexander and the intervention of the new power, Rome. Thanks to her foresight, Rhodes succeeded in advancing and protecting her economic interests. It became the most important centre of transit trade and therefore became very important to the economic life of Egypt. All merchant vessels from Mainland Greece, Asia Minor, the Black Sea and even from the ports of Phoenicia and Palestine, that were heading for Alexandria, called in at Rhodes. Phoenician traders had agencies there because Phoenician merchandise for S. Italy and Sicily, as well as goods from the West destined for Phoenician ports, all passed through Rhodes. At the same time, Rhodes continued to export; Rhodian amphoras, once filled with the much sought-after wine, have been found almost everywhere, as far as distant Mesopotamia and even Carthage. After the decline of Egypt in the last quarter of the 3rd century B.C., all the commercial traffic of the Aegean came essentially into the hands of the Rhodians. There were private banks on the island that even gave loans to other Greek cities. One source of Rhodes' power was the good organisation of its navy and its strong military and commercial fleet.

In 220 B.C. the Rhodians fought a successful war against Byzantion, which wanted to impose a tariff on the cereals leaving the Black Sea; according to Polybius, the Rhodians were recognised as "Rulers of the Seas" at this time.

Rhodes even managed to derive advantage from the terrible earthquake of 227/6 B.C., that resulted in the destruction of a large part of the city's defensive walls, houses and dockyards, and which also demolished the Colossus. Almost all the rulers and cities of the Hellenistic world sent aid, which was so great in total that the reconstructed city was even finer than before. The Colossus was not re-erected, since an oracle had circulated to the effect that if it were, it would cause great evil to the city; this was probably a shrewd invention of Rhodian propaganda, however, to enable them to use the money intended for the Colossus to strengthen their fleet.

At the end of the 3rd century B.C., Philip V of Macedonia decided to take advantage of the weakness of the Ptolemies and extend his power in the Aegean. Rhodes was one of his rivals in this area, and he therefore created problems for her by stirring up other powers against her, as well as the pirates. Rhodes defeated the pirates and declared war on Philip, in alliance with Attalos of Pergamon and Byzantion. This did not put an end to Philip's expansionist ambitions, however, and in 201 B.C. Rhodes and Attalos sent an embassy to Rome to denounce his activities. From that time on, Rhodes cooperated in combatting the enemies of Rome. As a result of her cooperation with the Romans in the war against Antiochus, the island extended both its influence and its territory. In the naval battle at Side (190 B.C.), the Rhodian forces, led by Eudamos, defeated Hannibal, who was at that point military adviser to Antiochus. After the final defeat of Antiochus III, a large part of Karia and Lycia were ceded to the Rhodians (188 B.C.). Rhodes extended its system of alliances to include many free cities in Asia Minor, controlled the Island League, and increased the weight of its coinage. Difficulties quickly arose, however; the Lycians demanded their independence, with the support of Rome, and the attitude adopted by Rhodes towards Perseus, the king of Macedonia, resulted in Rome removing Lycia and almost the whole of Karia from her control (167 B.C.). A year later, Rhodes suffered the greatest blow in its history when the Romans proclaimed Delos a free port. The revenue derived by Rhodes from the tax on goods in transit fell from 1,000,000 to 150,000 Rhodian drachmae.

12

12. Reconstruction of the Rhodes of the Knights at the beginning of the 16th century, when it reached the peak of its prosperity. It shows the marvellous defensive system, with its towers, gates and moat, that aroused such admiration in contemporary travellers who refer to it as "inexpugnabile". The Collachium, reserved exclusively for the residences of the Knights, was separ-

Decline of Rhodes — The Roman Period

In 164 B.C. the Romans concluded an alliance with the Rhodians, in accordance with which the island was obliged to take part in Roman military campaigns, even when these were directed against powers with which Rhodes was on friendly terms. Thus they assisted the Romans in the Third Punic War, which ended in the destruction of Carthage in 146 B.C., and also in the Mithridatic Wars between 88 and 63 B.C. Mithridates laid siege to Rhodes but failed to capture it.

In the war between Pompey and Julius Caesar (1st century B.C.) the Rhodians fought on the side of the loser, Pompey. Later, when Cassius, one of the Republicans who murdered Caesar, sought aid from them, the Rhodians waited on the decision of the Roman Senate before deciding to offer their support. Their prudence did not avail them on this occasion, however; Cas-

ated from the Burgum, the remainder of the city, by a second, inner line of defence works. Special attention was paid to the defence of the two harbours which were protected by the Saint Nicholas Tower, the Naillac Tower and the Tower of the Windmills. The entrance to the larger, commercial harbour could be closed by means of a heavy chain.

sius had studied on the island and knew it well, and therefore managed to capture it and bleed it dry of money, precious metals, works of art and ships (42 B.C.). Rome was then filled with Rhodian statues and Rhodes itself never recovered from the passage of Cassius. Augustus treated Rhodes well. He allowed it to retain its local autonomy, and made use of certain points of Rhodian maritime law. One law of Augustus made Rhodes a refuge for political exiles.

The island was shaken by a great earthquake in A.D. 142 and, despite all the assistance of Antoninus Pius, it failed to recover and sank back to the status of a provincial city in the vast Roman Empire. The next event of comparable impact was the raid by the Goths in A.D. 269. In A.D. 297 Rhodes became part of the province of the islands (*Provincia Insularum*) under the new administrative division of the Roman Empire.

Christianity spread early to Rhodes; at the end of the 4th century A.D. it became the "Metropolis" of the islands, with a number of bishops under its jurisdiction. According to tradition, the beginnings of the Church on Rhodes date from the period when the Apostle Paul called at the island on his journey from Miletos to Syria (A.D. 57).

Medieval Period

In the following period, the contemporary sources only mention Rhodes with reference to the various raids and natural disasters that befell it. There was a particularly destructive earthquake in A.D. 515, as a result of which the fortified city was restricted to what today is the area of the old city.

In the 7th century A.D. Rhodes was raided by the Persians of Khosroes (A.D. 620), and was captured for a number of years by the Arabs of Moa'wia who seized the ruins of the Colossus and sold them (A.D. 654). During the following century the island suffered destruction in the course of the Arab attack on Constantinople, and in the 9th century A.D. it was plundered by the Caliph of Baghdad, Arun al Raschid. The Turkish pirate Tzachas captured Rhodes in A.D. 1089, but was expelled from the island three years later by the Byzantine fleet.

The 11th century, with the concession of commercial privileges to the Venetians by Byzantium, saw the beginning of the direct and frequently destructive intervention of the West in the affairs of Rhodes. Byzantium attempted to remove these privileges in the 12th century, but the Venetians responded by plundering Rhodes and the other islands in the E. Aegean. Richard II the Lionheart and Philip II called at Rhodes on their way to the Holy Land in 1191, in order to procure provisions and mercenaries. When Constantinople was captured by the Crusaders in 1204 the lord of Rhodes, Leon Gavalas, made himself independent with the consent of the Venetians, assumed the title "Caesar" and struck his own coinage. Rhodes remained independent until the liberation of Constantinople from the Franks, and only occasionally recognised the authority of the Kingdom of Nicaea. Until 1309, when the island finally came into the hands of the Knights, it was governed by a variety of independent or almost independent rulers.

Period of the Knights

The Knights of St John ultimately decided to settle on the island of Rhodes, and captured it with the aid of the Genoese. The Order of the Knights of St John was founded in the 11th century and initially had religious aims, but, with the Crusades, it soon acquired a military character. When the Knights established themselves on Rhodes they created a new state to which were added the neighbouring islands of Nisyros, Telos,

Syme, Kos, Leros and Kalymnos. This meant that for a period of over 200 years Rhodes did not share the decline of the other provincial cities, since it was the capital of a small state, albeit a foreign one; it also avoided the fate of other areas of Greece which, one by one, became part of the Ottoman Empire. The subjection of Rhodes to foreign rulers led to conflicts, mostly centering around religious matters arising out of doctrinal differences. These conflicts, however, never assumed great dimensions, for they were over-shadowed by an aim common to both sides — the defence of the island against external danger.

The members of the Order of St John came from all the European Catholic countries and were divided into classes based on the degree of nobility of their origins and the services they had to offer as soldiers, nurses or clerics. The organisation was based on the country of origin, and the Knights were divided into seven *Tongues* or national groups: Provence, Auvergne, France, Italy, Germany, England and Spain, which was later divided into Aragon and Castile, raising the number of *Tongues* to eight. The administration of the Order and the new state was in the hands of the Grand Master, who held office for life, and an advisory body of the leaders *(piliers)* of the *Tongues*. Nineteen Grand Masters held office in the period 1309-1522, most of them of French extraction. The official languages of the Order were Latin and French. The fact that the Knights were a heterogeneous group in terms of racial origin meant that they were incapable of assimilating the local population either linguistically or politically, and they only intervened in questions of religious administration. Rhodes was obliged to sever its links with the Patriarchate and recognise the spiritual primacy of the Pope. The Order appointed a Latin archbishop, the *Archiepiscopus Colossensis* (the Rhodians were called Colossaeans, after the Colossus), to whom the bishop, who was known as the Greek rather than Orthodox bishop, was responsible. The Patriarchate continued to elect bishops, though the Order did not permit them to enter the state.

The characteristic features of this period are the threat from the Turks, which grew ever greater, the building activity of the Knights, which derived from the need to meet external dangers, and the increase in commercial activity consequent upon the establishment of European merchants on Rhodes.

In 1310, Ottoman, the ruler of the new Turkish state, laid siege to the island, but without success. Shortly afterwards his son, Prince Orhan, was defeated by the naval forces of the Knights.

When Mohammed II ascended the throne (1451), he renewed the treaties that had existed between his father and the Knights, but he later demanded that they should become his subjects and pay tax. These demands met with no response and in 1457 he sent a force to Rhodes which made a landing at Archangelos, plundered it and escaped.

A sharpening in the relations between the Order and the Venetians resulted in the pillaging of the interior of the island by the Venetian army. This was repeated a few years later by the Turks. Finally, Mohammed dispatched a large military force to the island under the leadership of Mesikh Pasha Palaiologos, a Greek renegade. The siege (1480) lasted three months and ended in the withdrawal of the Turks, after a large force (possibly

100,000) had failed to crush the resistance of the people and the 7000 Knights.

A year later, there was yet another destructive earthquake; the damage was quickly repaired, mainly involving the reconstruction of the defences under the supervision of the very competent Grand Master d'Aubusson (1476-1503). In 1498 Rhodes was visited by a plague which lasted for 18 months and wrought great damage. It is described by Emmanuel Georgilas in his poem *"The Plague of Rhodes"*.

With the accession to the throne of Suleiman the Magnificent (1522), the Ottoman Empire entered its period of greatest prosperity, and Rhodes' days were inevitably numbered. The siege of the island, which began on June 26th, 1522, is considered one of the most important military ventures of the period. The confrontation was singularly unequal; to oppose the 400 ships and 200,000 strong army of the Turks, the Knights had a total force of 5600, together with the fairly numerous, untrained populace. Suleiman himself arrived on July 28th. The struggle was a fierce one, but the besieged held out, despite lack of food and supplies, and in the face of espionage and treachery. In December it became apparent that continued resistance would mean ultimate destruction, and the surrender was arranged on fairly moderate terms. The Knights secured their withdrawal, with their arms and ships; a large number of Rhodians (4-5000) left with them. They all went to Crete as a temporary measure, and in the end the Knights established themselves on Malta. The Turkish losses were enormous (as high as 100,000).

The Turkish Occupation

Inspite of the privileges granted to them by the Turks (which were not always observed), Rhodes' position during the period of the Turkish occupation (1522-1912) was essentially one of subjugation. The rest of the Dodecanese, with the exception of Kos, fared much better, the difference in treatment being due to the fact that Rhodes and Kos had offered resistance. The privileges included freedom of religion and immunity from the forced levy of children. The Greeks, however, were driven out of the city, where they were permitted to engage in commercial activities, but not to dwell. The religious administration, in the person of the Metropolitan of Rhodes, acquired greater power and importance for the Greeks than before; he was the ethnarch and the president of the Council of Elders.

In 1658 Rhodes was attacked by the Venetian F. Morosini, the general who was responsible for the destruction of the Parthenon in Athens.

Lindos attained great economic prosperity during the period. An 18th-century traveller described it as a city, along with Rhodes, and adds that

13. A miniature illustration by the Knight Caoursin, depicting the city and the Turkish army besieging it in 1480. Paris, Bibliothèque Nationale.

there were 33 Greek and 5 Turkish villages on the island. In 1820 many of the dignitaries of the island, including the Metropolitan, became members of the *Philike Hetairia* (a secret organisation which aimed at the freeing of Greece from the Turks). Conditions did not permit the spread of the Greek War of Independence to the island, however, since it was a base for the Turkish army and the Egyptian fleet was continuously present.

The second half of the 19th century saw a number of disasters, such as the earthquakes of 1851, 1856 and 1862; the blowing up of the Knights' church of St John by gunpowder, which had lain hidden and forgotten in its cellars since the period of the Knights; and a fire in 1876 which destroyed a large number of Greek shops and which does not appear to have been accidental.

After the revolt of Crete, Turkish refugees settled on Rhodes. The proclamation of the Turkish constitution in 1908, contrary to expectation, was essentially an infringement of the island's privileges, according to which the *rayahs* could gain exemption from military service by paying a tax. Military service now became compulsory and this was the main reason for the mass emigration of young men, who went mainly to America.

The Italian Occupation

The Italian armies captured Rhodes and the rest of the Dodecanese in 1912, in order to cut Turkish communications with Tripoli, which was the object of Italian colonialist ambitions. The Italian occupation lasted until 1945, much longer than the inhabitants of the island expected; they had hoped that it would mark a short phase and that they would quickly be united with the Greek state. This created the "Dodecanese Question" with disorders and conflicts that resulted in mass arrests and deportations. In the Treaty of Lausanne (1923), Turkey ceded her rights in the islands to Italy, and the situation of the Greek population deteriorated with the rise of Fascism in Italy. In 1924 a programme of "Italianisation" of the population was instituted, involving the settlement on the island of Italians and the promotion of mixed marriages and the Italian language. The inhabitants of the islands were called "Orthodox" by the Italian administration, to avoid using the word "Greeks". The Italians also undertook works that benefitted the public, however, the most important of which was the road network; they also took an interest in modernising farming methods, founded the Museum and the Archaeological Service, conducted excavations and promoted Rhodes as a tourist centre. In 1936, De Vecchi, who had previously been Minister of Education and was one of Fascism's leading figures, was appointed General Administrator of the Dodecanese. His programme included the universal use of the Italian language; the use of Greek was forbidden in public places. The Germans took over in 1943, and finally surrendered in 1945. From this date, when the island was liberated, until 1947 and the signing of the peace between Italy and the Allies by which Italy ceded the

Dodecanese to Greece, Rhodes was administered by the British. In 1947 the Greek military administration assumed power and in the following year (March 1st, 1948) the Dodecanese was officially incorporated into the Greek State.

ART AND CULTURE

Literature

Rhodes was one of the seven cities that claimed to be the birthplace of Homer. That this claim cannot be substantiated is of little importance; from an early point in time the island produced a series of poets and men of wisdom and intellect that made it one of the most important cultural centres in ancient Greece. The epic poet Peisandros of Kamiros, who produced his *Herakleia* in the 7th century B.C., was the most famous poet after Homer and Hesiod. Kleoboulos, son of Euagoras, in addition to being a politician, was also a poet and one of the Seven Sages. He was the source of the apophthegm "the mean is the best". Later on, other poets became famous in their own time, such as Timokreon of Ialysos (beginning of the 5th century B.C.), and Anaxandrides of Kamiros (beginning of the 4th century B.C.). During the 3rd century B.C. the poet Apollonios of Rhodes, who was born in Alexandria or Naukratis, lived on Rhodes and wrote a great number of works, of which the only one to survive is the *Argonautica* (5834 lines), an epic poem that was very popular in antiquity.

From the 4th century B.C. onwards Rhodes began to attract distinguished foreigners, who stayed there for a period of time, or even for the rest of their lives. Amongst them was the philosopher Aristippos of Cyrene, a pupil of Socrates. Eudemos of Rhodes, one of the best pupils of Aristotle, introduced the peripatetic philosophy to Rhodes; he also concerned himself with mathematics. It is also said that Aeschines, the Athenian orator, settled on Rhodes and founded a school of rhetoric (4th century B.C.). From the end of the 2nd century B.C. onwards, there was an exceptional flowering of the intellectual life of the island, and Rhodes became, after Athens, the most important centre of higher education in the Hellenistic world. Panaitios of Rhodes, who came from Kamiros, was one of the great figures in Stoicism, and founded the Middle Stoa, a landmark in the history of Stoicism. One of his pupils was Poseidonios of Apameia, who eventually settled and taught on Rhodes. Panaitios became famous for his studies in astronomy and philology, while Poseidonios wrote history and also studied physics, mathematics and geography. The Rhodian grammatical schools were also famous. The philosopher and grammarian Dionysios of Thrace, known for his work *The Art of Grammar,* was one of the many people who taught on Rhodes at this time.

The rhetorical schools in particular flourished, and many distinguished Romans, the most outstanding of whom was Cicero, attended the lessons taught at them.

The natural sciences, astronomy, geography, physics, mathematics and medicine were cultivated on Rhodes.

Art

Rhodes became a centre of artistic activity from a very early date. A visit to the Archaeological Museum is both agreeable and instructive, and brings one into contact with the works of art produced on the island from the Mycenaean to the Roman period. The main features are missing from the picture that we can form today of this artistic productivity; during the period of the island's prosperity these were, in addition to their quality, the great size, the brilliance and the large numbers of the works which decorated Rhodes at that time. The great artists, sculptors and painters whose names have survived – those of the architects have not – are known to us because their reputation has found its place in the written tradition; the names of a few of the sculptors are preserved on the bases of statues now lost, and just few of their works survive in copies dating from the Roman period. Not a single painting has survived. The names of over 100 artists from the last four centuries B.C. are known only from inscriptions. Many of them were Rhodians, but at the same time many foreigners from the coast of Asia Minor or from the rest of Greece worked in this important artistic centre. A brief enumeration of their works may perhaps give a faint idea of the contribution of Rhodes to the history of art. The synoecism of Rhodes in 408 B.C. marked a turning point in the intellectual and artistic life of the island; it was mainly from this date that the Rhodians began to invite distinguished creative artists to work here or to buy their works.

The great Classical painter Parrhasios of Ephesos, known chiefly for his work in Athens (middle of the 5th to the beginning of the 4th century B.C.), worked on Rhodes, where he produced a painting of Herakles at Lindos and of the three heroes Meleagros, Herakles and Perseus at Rhodes itself.

Bryaxis of Athens (middle of the 4th century B.C.), one of the four sculptors who worked on the Mausoleum of Halikarnassos, carved five colossal statues of gods on Rhodes.

Lysippos of Sikyon, the sculptor whom Alexander the Great chose to produce his portraits, set up one of his most famous works on Rhodes – the bronze *quadriga* with the god Helios. At the same period the people of Rhodes dedicated a similar work, the gold chariot of Helios, at Delphi, the base of which is preserved. Deinokrates, the architect of Alexander the Great, who drew up the plans for Alexandria, also appears to have been a Rhodian.

The great painter Protogenes from Kaunos in Karia lived and worked on Rhodes for the most part. During the siege of Demetrios, Protogenes con-

14. The Victory of Samothrace, one of the most famous pieces of Rhodian art, was dedicated by the Rhodians in the Sanctuary of the Kabeiroi on Samothrace after their victory over Antiochus in 190 B.C. Paris, Louvre.

14

tinued work on his painting of Ialysos (on which he worked for a total of 7 or 11 years) in his studio outside the walls. When Demetrios asked him how it was that he was not afraid, he replied that he was aware that the king was at war with the Rhodians, not with the arts. Some of his works adorned the *Dionysion* on Rhodes, while others that are known are the *Resting Satyr,* a portrait of Antigonos, Demetrios' father, etc.

After the unsuccessful siege by Demetrios, the Colossus, perhaps the most renowned statue in antiquity, was set up on Rhodes; it was a statue of Helios and was one of the seven wonders of the world. Its creator was Chares of Lindos, a pupil of Lysippos, and it is said to have taken twelve years to complete. Some impression of the Colossus may be derived from the coins of the island and from later imaginary reconstructions of it, and the fact that it was said to be 31m. high. Pliny, who saw it after it had collapsed during the earthquake of 227/6 B.C., states that it was only with difficulty that one could put one's arms round the thumb. The site on which the statue stood is not known with certainty; legend has it that it straddled the entrance to the harbour and that the ships sailed under its legs. The most plausible view is that it stood in the precinct of the temple of Helios, on the site now occupied by the Grand Master's palace. The Arabs of Moa'wia sold the bronze from it to a Syrian merchant on the coast opposite, and 900 camels were needed to take it away. Pliny relates that there were another hundred colossoi on Rhodes, which demonstrates how fond the citizens were of enormous works of art, and also how wealthy.

The sculptor Boethos is known for his works in the sanctuary of Athena Lindia in the 2nd century B.C.; amongst originals from this century that have been attributed to Rhodian workshops we may note a bronze *Sleeping Eros* (New York, Metropolitan Museum) and the *Victory of Samothrace* (Louvre), one of the finest surviving pieces of Greek art. It was dedicated by the Rhodians in the sanctuary of the Kabeiroi on Samothrace, after their victory over Antiochus III in 190 B.C., and was probably a work of Pythokritos, who also carved a boat in relief on the rock at Lindos. Victory is standing on her right foot on the prow of a boat that forms the base of the statue.

The artistic school of Rhodes from the 2nd century B.C. onwards, is considered to have been one of the most important in the Hellenistic period. The *Laokoön group* (Vatican Museum) was admired both in antiquity and in the Renaissance period (it was discovered in 1506). Michelangelo refused to undertake its restoration, fearing that he would be unable to reproduce the quality of the original. It was created by three Rhodian sculptors: Hagesandros, Polydoros and Athenodoros, and the generally accepted date for it is the middle of the 2nd century B.C. There is a copy of it in the Palace of the Grand Master.

15. The statue of Laokoön, another world famous Rhodian work of art. It depicts Laokoön and his sons, locked in the deadly embrace of the monstrous serpents sent by Apollo. Vatican Museum.

THE CITY OF RHODES AND ITS MONUMENTS

The Ancient City

Considerable light has been shed by the excavations of the Greek Archaeological Service, and by the earlier Italian excavations, on the picture of
ancient Rhodes that one gains from the sources and a simple account of the
works of art that once adorned it. The splendid public and private buildings
with which the city was once embellished have been lost along with the
works of art. It has proved possible, however, at least to establish the sites
of some of them, as well as the dimensions and street-plan of the city. A
city that has been occupied without interruption for 2500 years, and which
has experienced the violence of nature (earthquakes and floods) and suffered repeated destructions from sieges and plundering, presents a very difficult problem for archaeology. The discoveries consist simply of the foundations of buildings, which are difficult to identify, and of sections of the
defensive walls, or ancient building material that has been re-used at a later
date. Occasionally mosaic floors are found, and sculptures which have also
been used as building material. The gaps in the finds are supplemented by
references in the ancient authors. The construction of the city commenced in
408 B.C., based on the plan of Hippodamos of Miletos, the greatest town-
planner in the ancient world, or one of his pupils. The system used in
Rhodes was to divide the city up into a grid consisting of regular rectangles;
this was achieved not only by the street plan, with series of parallel roads
intersecting at right angles, but also by the initial division of the space to be
occupied by the city on the basis of a specific metric unit. The result was a
logical predetermined creation. The whole area was divided into zones cor-
responding to the various aspects of the city's life – public buildings, commercial quarter, residences etc. The roads were oriented E-W and N-S and
the width of them varied from 5-16 m. The acropolis was on the W. side of
the city at a point above it; it had no special defence works and had many
levelled areas and groves, according to an ancient description. The population at the period of the city's greatest prosperity (3rd and 2nd centuries
B.C.), is calculated to have been 60-100,000.

The reconstruction of the city-plan is based on the study of the streets of
the medieval and later cities, and on aerial photography, as well as on the
results of archaeological investigation. These techniques have established
that many of the later streets overlay the ancient ones; these include the
Street of the Knights in the medieval town, which led from the ancient
acropolis to the "Great Harbour", the present day commercial harbour. Traces of the moles of both the "Great" and the "Lesser" harbour (Mandraki) are
still preserved beneath the modern moles of St Nicholas and the Windmills.
Mandraki was the military harbour and could be closed with chains; it was
also the site of the dockyards *(neoria)*. The other three harbours appear to
have been ancillary; no traces have been found of two of them, and the third
was the harbour of Akantia. The *Deigma* was near the modern commercial
harbour; this was the market place and was located near the agora. The ex-

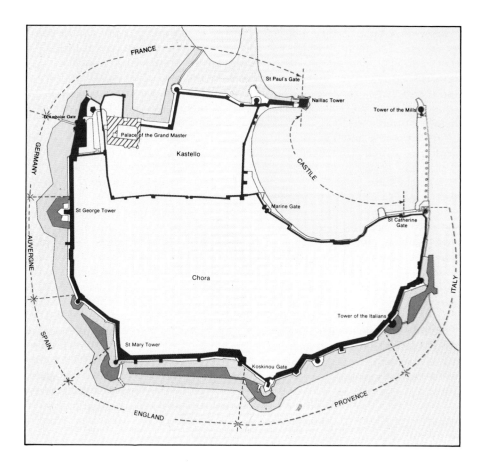

16. The drawing shows the plan of the walls and the moat, the gates, the towers, and the very strictly defined positions assigned to each of the "Tongues" in the defence of the city. The moat and the earthworks are marked in different colours.

act location of these buildings has not yet been determined, and this is also true of the *Dionysion* which housed the works of art, though this must also have been in the centre. The only surviving remains of the buildings in the area near the commercial harbour belong to a small **temple of Aphrodite,** on the NE edge of the medieval town opposite the Freedom Gate, built in the 3rd century B.C., of which the foundations and a few architectural members are preserved.

The ancient acropolis was on the hill of Aghios Stefanos, known as *Monte Smith,* after the English admiral who established an observation post there in 1802. It was excavated and restored by the Italians. The ruins of the temple of **Athena Polias and Zeus Polieus** stand on the northernmost point of the hill. The temple, which has an E-W orientation, was one of the city's most important sanctuaries; it was here that the colossal statue of the *Populus Romanus* (14 m. high) was erected in 163 B.C. The rock-hewn structures with niches for votive offerings, to the NE and W. of the temple, were connected with the underground water conduits of the city. They were perhaps **Nymphaia** – where the Nymphs were worshipped.

Further to the south there is a group of buildings that formed one of the centres of Rhodian intellectual and artistic life. The highest site to the west is occupied by the large **temple of Pythian Apollo,** which is approached by a large staircase. A section of it has been restored. Below and to the east of the temple lies the **Stadium,** which has been restored, only a few of the rows in the centre of the curve being ancient (2nd century B.C.). A little to the north of the entrance to the stadium there is a small **Theatre,** which is also restored; only 2 or 3 seats in the front row and a few steps of the left-hand staircase are genuine. Its dimensions (only 27 m. x 23 m.) and its capacity (only 800 spectators) demonstrate that this was not the main theatre of the ancient city; it will have been used for musical or other events held in honour of Apollo, and the fact that it is situated near the stadium and the gymnasium has given rise to the suggestion that it was an amphitheatre in which the Rhodian teachers of rhetoric gave their lessons. Just to the east of the stadium lay the **Gymnasium,** of which little has survived. Though there are few remains on the ancient acropolis, the site affords a wonderful view; to the west Syme and the coast of Asia Minor can be seen in the distance, while the city spreads out to the north and east. The temples on the acropolis will have been visible to travellers approaching from the sea, and Strabo wrote of Rhodes in the 1st century A.D. that there was none finer than it, or even its equal.

To the southwest of the stadium there are tombs and remains of the outer wall of the city. Parts of the defensive wall have also been found at many other points. The drainage and water systems have also been discovered; these are works of amazing perfection which were constructed for the most part when the city was founded. The architectural forms of private houses exhibit great variety; many of them were large and the floors of the main rooms were covered with mosaics (some of which are now in the Archaeological Museum). The cemeteries were on the south side of the city. The necropoleis of the 4th and 3rd centuries B.C. have been excavated near Rhodini. Many of the tombs were dug into the rock, the most impressive of them being the one erroneously called the **tomb of the Ptolemies,** an imposing monument with sides 27.80 m. long and originally 5 m. high.

The Medieval City to the Period of the Knights

The end of the ancient world did not see the end of the prosperity of the city; the Early Christian finds from all over the island demonstrate that, on the contrary, both the economic and intellectual life of the island must have continued on a high level. New discoveries are continually adding to the number of Early Christian churches on the island. The finds in the city come from the area corresonding with the SW part of the ancient city on the lower slopes of the acropolis; amongst them is the **basilica** uncovered in recent years at the intersection of the streets Cheimarras and P. Mela. This is a very large building, up to 60 m. long, with mosaic floors dated to the middle of the 5th century A.D. This period of the city is further represented by another building with mosaics in th same area (Cheimarras street), and a basilica on the site of the new stadium; to these should be added the numerous architectural members that may be found in the Archaeological Museum, incorporated into buildings of the Knights, or used in Byzantine churches of a later date. The earthquake of A.D. 515 was the main cause of their destruction, and also resulted in the city being confined within the limits of the subsequent medieval town.

` The raids of the following centuries brought nothing but destruction to Rhodes. Byzantine fortresses were built on the island during the 7th century. Several churches were built during the period of the Gavalas family in the 13th century, and the establishment of the rule of the Knights did not put a stop to their construction or produce any significant change in their architectural style. On the contrary, the Byzantine tradition was continued. The churches of the city were situated within the walled town, and after the Turkish conquest they were all converted into mosques. The Greek inhabitants were compelled by the conquerors to reside outside the walls, and they began to build their new churches in the new quarters that came into being. The medieval town is very densely built up, with narrow labyrinthine alleys, and it is difficult to locate some of the monuments referred to below. Apart from its main streets, however, it still offers the visitor the chance to escape from the crowd, and follow his own whim while becoming acquainted with it; often one may lose one's way and arrives at a point other than that intended, but this never induces disappointment, since one has gained knowledge of one more corner of this unique city, which is small enough to make losing one's way a pleasant experience. Out of the total of 15 monuments mentioned below, the most interesting are the church of Our Lady of the Castle (Panaghia tou Kastrou), the Monastery of Aghios Georgios (Hurmali Medrese), Aghios Fanourios, Archangelos Michail (Demirli), Aghia Triada (Dolapli) and Aghia Ekaterini (Ilk Mihrab).

Our **Lady of the Castle** (Panaghia tou Kastrou), a large church with a cross-in-square plan, is the first Byzantine church encountered as one enters the old town through the Freedom Gate, having walked as far as the Archaeological Museum. The building of this church commenced in the 11th or 12th century and in all probability it remained unfinished or collapsed as the result of an earthquake. Construction of it was later resumed in the Gothic style (roof and windows) after the arrival of the Knights, and it became the Catholic Cathedral Our Lady of the Castle (Panaghia tou Kastrou). It has a number of Byzantine frescoes as well as some Frankish ones of the

14th century. The Turks converted it into a mosque, and called it *Ederum* or *Kaduri*.

To the west of the mosque of Suleiman, in Apollonion street, there is a church which has great architectural interest, being originally the *katholikon* of a Byzantine monastery of **Aghios Georgios** (built in the 14th century). A narthex and a portico with Gothic features, were added to the north side of the original tetraconch (four-apsed) plan (15th century). The church is known as **Hurmali Medrese,** meaning "School of the Date Palm", because it was converted into a Turkish theological school. In the same area, just to the north, is the small cruciform church of **Aghios Markos,** known as Sadri-Gelebi, while another church, with the same plan, of **Aghia Paraskevi,** (Takkedji Mosque), lies to the south in Ippodamou street. This area also has a small three-aisled basilica, which is broader than it is long and has three entrances. It is known as **Kadi Mestzid,** and has frescoes dating from the end of the 14th or beginning of the 15th century. To the south, in a side-street off Ippodamou street, is the Monastery of **Aghios Nikolaos** (Abdul Tzelil Mosque, also called the Tsiukur cami), a two-aisled basilica with a large number of Gothic features, including a portico on the N. side of the building, dating from the 15th century. The church is earlier in date and at a lower level; there is a staircase leading to it from the portico. The southern end of Ippodamou street leads to the district of the Gate of St Athanasios; to the left of this is the small one-aisled church of the same name, which is also known as Bab-u-Mestud (mosque of the closed gate). There is another one-aisled church of **Aghia Kyriaki,** just to the east, with an entrance on the N. side. This is called Alemnak Mestzid (building of the standard-bearer), and, according to the Turkish tradition was founded by Suleiman's standard-bearer. Further still to the east is a small one-aisled basilica of **Archangelos Michail** (Hudai Mestzid).

The church of Aghios Fanourios is in Aghios Fanourios street, squeezed between the houses on either side of it; nowadays it forms one of the parishes of the old town. It was at one stage a mosque with the name of *Peial-el-din.* It is a small 13th-century church in the form of a cross, with two layers of frescoes preserved, which apparently depicted the same subjects; more of the later layer can be made out. We may note the 18 angels on the dome and the 16 prophets between the windows of it. The rest of the decoration includes the Crucifixion, with the Virgin Mary and St. John the Baptist on the E. side of the S. arch; Salome carrying on her head a plate bearing the head of John the Baptist, on the E. side of the N. arch; and the large portrait of the archangel Gabriel on the northern wall (in accordance with the prevailing practice on Rhodes, the archangels Michael and Gabriel are depicted on a very large scale. The south apse has a scene showing the founder offering a model of the church to Christ, and an inscription dating the renovation of it to 1335/36.

17. Reconstruction of the mole, the Naillac Tower and the Gate of St Paul. The tower was very skilfully designed. It was square in section, with a small octagonal tower on top of it ringed by four circular turrets. The entrance to the harbour could be closed by a chain binding the Naillac Tower and the Tower of the Windmills.

A little way to the north, in a side street off Aghios Fanourios street, is the church of **Aghios Spyridon** (Kavakli Mestzid), a basilica with cupole. To the NE of Kavakli is a large cross-in-square church of **Archangelos Michail** (Domirli Mosque), which bears some resemblance to Our Lady of the Castle. It was damaged by a bomb during the last war. Founded in the 14th century, it later had a Gothic portico added to it, and probably became the cathedral for the Greeks when the Knights made the church of Our Lady their own. Some frescoes are preserved. In the SE area of the old town, not far from the Gate of Koskinou, there are two interesting churches which also became mosques; **Aghia Triada** (Dolapli Mosque) which originally had the shape of a cross, with later additions and Gothic details in its decoration. It dates from the middle of the 15th century. The frescoes have faded to a considerable degree, the ones on the western arch being later.

The other church in this area is that of **Aghia Ekaterini,** known as *Ilk Mihrab,* which means the first niche for prayer; according to a Turkish tradition it was the first Christian church in which Suleiman prayed after his entry into the city. It has three aisles, with vaults of equal height, that take the form of pediments on the façade, and frescoes from the 14th and 15th centuries. Finally, there is the church **of Aghios Panteleimon,** near the Gate of St Catherine, at the NE end of the fortifications. It is in the form of a half-inscribed cross and was built to commemorate the victory over the Turks during the siege of 1480. Today it is a parish church.

Rhodes During the Period of the Knights

Of all the periods of the city's history, the occupation of the Knights left the most permanent mark upon it, and, despite its short duration, gave to it the enduring character of a 15th-century city. The medieval city is in a wonderful state of preservation, even though 500 years have elapsed since it was completed. It preserves very few traces of the Turkish presence, which lasted 390 years, because the Turks found ample buildings to serve their purposes and did not have to build any new ones, apart from a number of mosques. The other buildings were easily converted into Turkish places of worship, by the addition of a minaret or a fountain, or into residences by adding a covered wooden balcony or wooden grilles at the windows. Many of the minarets were demolished after the end of the Turkish occupation, and the sections that had been added to the state buildings of the period of the Knights, in order to convert them into residences, were removed. There is thus little testimony to the passage of the Turks, though the view of the city from a distance, or from any point outside the walls gains added grace and delicacy from the tall slender minarets. The Italian occupation had a positive effect on the medieval town at least, in spite of all the doubt and criticism surrounding the accuracy of their restorations, especially in the case of the Palace of the Grand Master.

The buildings of the Knights were in the Gothic style that had emerged in the 14th and 15th centuries in Provence, with the Papal Court at Avignon, in Spain and in Italy, though with some slight variations. On Rhodes the style remained more conservative, and did not follow the development it had in the other countries in which it flourished, where it developed the late Gothic form called *flamboyant.* A few features of the Renaissance made a belated appearance on the island around the year 1500.

The architecture of the Knights is divided by scholars into two periods:

18. *Reconstruction of the northwest side of the city walls, the d'Amboise gate and the palace of the Grand Master. The palace was a 14th-century building which had its own defence works, and acted as a bastion as well as the residence of the Grand Master on the northwest side of the Collachium.*

during the first (1309-1480) local craftsmen were employed, and some Byzantine elements were retained, but their creations did not attain the technical perfection of their Western models. The second period resulted from the needs caused by the destructions that occurred during the siege of Mohammed II (1480) and the earthquakes of 1481. This phase, which was of necessity much shorter than the first (1480-1522), was very productive, and the work was of a higher aesthetic quality, since it was all based on a predetermined building plan, under the supervision of the Grand Master d'Aubusson, himself an engineer; many Western architects and craftsmen, more-over, came specifically to offer their assistance. It was at this time that al-most all the important buildings in the mediveal town, including the de-fensive walls, were either built or repaired.

The fortified town, which includes the commercial harbour, is divided into two parts: the *Castellum* or *Collachium* is the northernmost, smaller part and was separated from the rest of it, the *Burgum*, by a wall. It formed the administrative centre and was the place where the Knights had their res-idences, while the *Burgum*, which included the commercial centre of the city, was the residence of the Greeks, the Jews and the Westerners who had settled on Rhodes.

Castellum or Collachium. The visitor to the northern part of the medi-eval town enters by the Freedom Gate, which is the only gate that did not form part of the original plan; it was opened by the Italians in 1924 in order to facilitate the flow of traffic. The visitor crosses Symis square, with the temple of Aphrodite on his left, and the first building he then comes to is the **"Inn" of the "Tongue" of Auvergne** (15th century, completed in 1507). Each of the *Tongues* into which the Knights were divided had an *Inn*, which was the social centre for the members of the group, and in which their of-ficers resided. As with other buildings of this type, the storerooms were in the basement and had a series of vaults in front of them. One peculiar fea-ture of this "Inn" is a stairway on the right side leading to a gallery that af-forded access to the first floor. The building exhibits the basic features com-mon to all edifices of this period, which produce an overall effect of an imposing mass, interrupted by very few openings for doors or windows, or by other architectural decoration. To the right, before one reaches its main façade, there is a small square with a font arranged as a fountain, (originally part of the baptistry of the Early Christian church of Aghia Irini at Arnitha) and piles of cannonballs from the siege of 1522. Facing on to Argyrokastro square is a building that today houses the offices of the Archaeological Ser-vice and the Library of the Historical and Archaeological Institute of the Dodecanese. It served a similar purpose during the Italian occupation, while the Turks, like the Knights, had used it as an arsenal. The building, one of the earliest in the *Collachium* (14th century), was originally the **First Hospital of the Knights,** and appears to have been built by the Grand Mas-ter R. de Pins (1355-65), whose coat of arms is on its façade.

Next to the "Inn" of Auvergne is the church of our Lady of the Castle (Panaghia tou Kastrou), and immediately beyond it, a small square in which is the main entrance to the **New Hospital of the Knights.** Opposite this is the **"Inn" of the "Tongue" of England** which also fronts onto this square; this was rebuilt in 1919 on the same site and with the same plan as the old building which was destroyed. Construction of the large, imposing Hospital began in 1440, and was completed considerably later when d'Au-busson was Grand Master (1476-1503). The entrance to it is a pointed door in one of the arches at ground level, that opens into a large interior court-yard (there is a smaller one to the south), consisting of a square surrounded by arcades. A staircase on the left leads to the upper floor. A number of rooms open into the arcade on this floor, amongst them the large ward for the sick, a chapel, and the dining room for the staff. The exterior surface of the middle side of the conch of the side chapel, exactly above the entrance to the building, incorporates a relief depicting two angels beneath the flag of the Order, holding the coat of arms of Grand Master de Lastic, or perhaps that of his predecessor Fluvian; according to the inscription beneath the relief he had left 10,000 florins for the construction of the *hospice*, the Greek name for which (*xenodocheion*) must derive from the form of the building, which is similar to that of the hostelries (*xenones*) of the Byzantine period. The Hospital of the Knights nowadays houses the Rhodes Archaeological Museum.

The **Street of the Knights** is perhaps the finest section of the Knights' city, and is certainly the most interesting for the study of buildings of this period. It begins at the Hospital and runs west to the highest point of the *Collachium*, which is the site of the Palace of the Grand Master (also called *Castello*). It overlies the ancient road, but the E. section of it, which led to the harbour, fell into disuse during the period of the Knights. The N. side of the Hospital faces onto this street, as well as a series of "Inns" and other important buildings. Opposite the side of the New Hospital, beyond the building on the corner, which is now a bank, is the **"Inn" of the "Tongue" of Italy,** built during the period when the Grand Master was an Italian, Del Carretto (1513-1521); his coat of arms may be seen on the façade. The next building on the same side of the road is a small palace, the façade of which incorporates, amongst other things, the coat of arms of the Grand Master d' Amboise, and the date 1505, as well as that of the last Grand Master, de l'Isle Adam, and the date 1521. The large side entrance to the Hospital is immediately opposite, and next to it is the **"Inn" of the "Tongue" of France,** a large building and the finest of all the "Inns" Its façade is more ornamented than those of the others, and it has a special feature in the four large windows on the first floor with the half "frames" carved in relief around the upper part of them. The coat of arms of Grand Master d'Amboise above the entrance stands out amongst the many carved on the façade. Between two of the first floor windows may be seen the escutcheon of France and the coat of arms of Grand Master d'Aubusson, with the date 1495. The building was probably completed at the beginning of the 16th century. At the point where the "Inn" of the "Tongue" of France ends, there is a side street down which is the small one-aisled **church of Aghios Dimitrios.**

Further along the Street of the Knights, and on the same side, there is a small 14th-century church of Aghia Triada (Holy Trinity), which was converted into a mosque called **Han-Zande.** This is followed by the building in which the sacristan of the church lived; both buildings were attached to the "Inn" of the "Tongue" of France. Immediately beyond them, a high arch bridges the street, followed by the **"Inn" of the "Tongue" of Provence,** while the **"Inn" of the "Tongue" of Spain** rises on the left, immediately after Ipparchou street; the former has points of similarity with the "Inn" of the "Tongue" of France, while the latter is a simpler, earlier building. The Street of the Knights terminated in a **loggia** consisting of a series of *ogee arches,* which originally connected the Palace with the **church of St John** opposite on the left of the street. The great explosion of 1856 destroyed the church and most of the loggia. The church of the protector of the Order, which was Gothic and three-aisled, was built during the first half of the 14th century, and the Grand Masters were buried in it (the grave reliefs of two of the Grand Masters are in the Cluny Museum in Paris and there are others in the Rhodes Archaeological Museum). The church built by the Italians at Mandraki, which is today that of the Annunciation, is a copy on a smaller scale of that of St John, the original site of which was later occupied by a Turkish school. Most of the loggia is restored.

The **Palace of the Grand Master** had suffered destruction even before this explosion and had been used as a prison by the Turks. It is a large (75 x 80 m.), impressively fortified building and its enormous storerooms housed the grain that the city needed in case it was blockaded. The building to be seen today has basically the same features as the 14th-century original, although it departs considerably from its model. It was restored in 1940, when De Vecchi was in charge of the administration of the Dodecanese, and was intended to be the residence of Victor Emmanuel and Mussolini on the occasions of their official visits. The Palace was therefore intentionally made more grandiose than the original, though the fact that it became quite an amusing building was an unintentional side effect. The great pointed door between the two round towers, is one of the parts preserved from the original building, and bears some similarity to the fine Sea Gate. Inside the door is a large covered area, on the left of which is the entrance to the main building, while straight ahead it opens into an interior courtyard surrounded by arches. There are various statues in these, which were brought from elsewhere when the building was reconstructed. To the right of the entrance there is an inscription in Italian referring to the 1940 reconstruction: "In the 18th year of the era of Fascism". Today the building functions as a **museum.** It is worth visiting not only for the mosaic floors brought from elsewhere to adorn it, but also for another important reason: the view of the old town from the many windows of the Palace is not simply a very fine one, but helps one to grasp the relations of the different buildings to each other. The Palace gardens also afford a splendid view. The windows, with the benches on both sides of them, are convenient places from which to dwell at leisure on the different views of the city. The mosaics have been laid on the floors of the large rooms, which are decorated with a variety of other, heterogeneous elements; coloured marbles, statues (including the copy of the Laokoön), Italian furniture, carpets on the walls, Chinese vases and so on. The mosaics, most of them transported from Kos, are Roman and Early Christian in date. Many of them consist of a combination, or a repeated series, of one or more abstract or schematised decorative motifs, while some of them portray specific subjects, such as the Medusa, the hunter striking a leopard, the nine Muses etc.

When one leaves the Palace and proceeds in a westerly direction, one can see the outer wall of the old town, and part of the inner wall that separated the *Collachium* from the *Burgum*. Near the SW corner of the Palace is the

Cannon Gate, from which a drawbridge leads west to the circuit of the defence wall.

Burgum. The visitor may see the buildings dating from the period of the Knights in the rest of the old town at the same time as he visits the Byzantine and Turkish monuments. The building near the Sea Gate of the harbour is the **"Kastellania"**, which served as a gathering point for merchants, the office of the market inspectorate and a merchants' court (*Basilica Mercatorum*) (*c.* 1500). The "Kastellania", like the "Inn" of the "Tongue" of Auvergne, has an outside staircase leading to the terrace, a feature that is thought to represent the influence of Aegean architecture. Proceeding to the E., one arrives in front of the building known as the **"Admiralty"**, which was in reality a large 15th-century aristocratic mansion, that was probably the residence of the Orthodox Metropolitan of Rhodes. The building overlooks the square of the Jewish Martyrs, which lies at the entrance to the old Jewish quarter. In the centre of the façade there is an inscription in Latin, which is repeated, in ancient Greek, in the courtyard: "Peace to this house and to all who dwell in it". Continuing to the E., the visitor comes upon the remains of Our Lady of the Burg (Panaghia tou Bourgou), which was the largest Catholic church on Rhodes. Near this is the **St Catherine Hospice,** which was administered by the "Tongue" of Italy. Finally, at the eastern edge of the city, there are preserved a few ruins of a Gothic church of **Our Lady of Victory** (Panaghia tes Nikes), built by the Grand Master d'Aubusson after the siege of 1480; the same courtyard contains the church of **Aghios Panteleimon,** also built after the victory over the Turks. Nearby is the St Catherine Gate, which is usually called the **Gate of the Windmills.**

The Walls. The final fortification of Rhodes took place in the years between the two sieges by the Turks in 1480 and 1522. It was during this period that the defence walls took the form they now have, though the Knights turned their attention to the completion and repair of them immediately after they settled on the island. D'Aubusson, however, concerned himself more than any of the other Grand Masters with the strengthening of the walls, and his coat of arms may be seen at 50 different points on them. At this period a number of alterations were made that rendered the town more capable of resisting the pounding of cannon-fire, and also of returning it. Most of the square towers were replaced by round ones for this purpose. The moat around the walls, which is as wide as 40 m., never filled with water, since it is above sea level, but it was fringed by a strong high earthwork. At certain points there was a double moat with earthworks in between the two ditches. There was a road circling the top of the wall, protected by a breastwork, and in some places there was a second path halfway up the wall which enabled the defenders to strike at their attackers from closer quarters. The fortifications of the old town comprised the defence wall on the mainland, the harbour wall, and the fortified moles of the harbour. Each *Tongue* of the Order was assigned a position at which it had to defend the walls. The amount of time and energy at the disposal of the visitor will determine whether he views the walls by walking around their external perimeter, in which case he will have greater opportunity to admire their construction, the Gates, and the countless coats of arms built into the walls, or whether he contents himself with visiting some of the Gates as he wanders through the streets of the town. There is yet another way, however; he may walk the circuit road on the wall itself, in which case he will be able to see the positions of the *Tongues*, the towers and the defence works below his feet, as well as gain a bird's eye view of the city. This tour takes place on certain days and at certain hours with the accompaniment of a guide; information at the Palace of the Grand Master.

The walls have a perimeter of 4 kms, the maximum length of the town being 1000 m. E-W and 800 m. N-S. The enceinte has the following **Gates:** that of **d'Amboise,** in the NW side is dated to 1512 and is protected by two huge circular towers; that of **St Athanasios** in the SW corner; according to Turkish tradition, this gate was closed by Suleiman after he had entered the city through it, so that no-one else could enter and capture it. In the S. section is the **Koskinou Gate** or **St John Gate.** The interior façade of this belongs to the earliest fortification period; later a second ditch was added, and the new gate with the coats of arms of d'Aubusson and the Order, as well as a relief depicting St John (now destroyed). On the E. side is the **Gate of St Catherine** or **of the Windmills,** the latter name deriving from a row of 13 windmills that stood on the mole at that period (three of them are preserved today). The **Sea Gate** in the middle of the harbour is the finest of them all. Above the semi-circular arch on the exterior of it there is a relief of the Virgin Mary between St John and St Peter, and the coat of arms of d'Aubusson, with the date 1478. The door is protected by two slightly curved towers. On the NW edge of the harbour, the **Tarsana Gate** connected the Dockyard, which was within the walls, with the harbour, and a short way to the north, the **Gate of St Paul** afforded communication with the **Naillac Tower** which stood on the end of the mole (it was destroyed in the 19th century). There were also a large number of other towers near to and in between the Gates of the walled town. We may note the **Tower of Spain,** outside the W. wall; the **Tower of the Virgin** near the Gate of St Athanasios and the **Tower of Italy,** a stout building on the E. side bearing the coat of arms of the Grand Master Del Carretto and the dates 1515-17. Finally the harbour was protected by, in addition to the square, 46 m. high **Naillac Tower,** built by the Grand Master of that name (1396-1421), a round tower opposite the Mole of the Windmills. The commercial harbour could be closed by a thick chain slung between the Naillac Tower and that on the Mole of the Windmills. Mandraki was protected by a very strong **Tower** of **St Nicholas** at the end of the Mole with the three windmills. The tower belonging to this fort was built by the Grand Master Zacosta in 1464-67, and a polygonal battlement was added around its moat by d'Aubusson after 1480.

The Turkish Monuments

The building activity of the Turks was in no way proportionate to the great length of the Turkish occupation (1523-1912). If one wished to point to some positive aspect of the Turkish presence on the island, it would be the respect they showed for the architectural form of the city they had captured. We may note the most important mosques of the medieval town. The first to be built, immediately after the conquest of Rhodes, was the **Mosque of Suleiman.** In 1808 the mosque, which today can be seen at the end of Sokratous street, was erected on the same site. Like all the other mosques, it has a courtyard with a fountain in which the faithful washed. Earlier material was used in the construction of it. The **Mosque of Ibrahim Pasha,** was built in 1531; it is the earliest of all, but has been considerably modified by later additions (such as the minaret). The **Mosque of Redjeb Pasha,** which looks onto a square with a fountain to the east of Aghios Fanourios, was built in 1588, and was the most imposing of all the Turkish buildings. The exterior of it was decorated with Persian tiles, resembling the plates of Lindos, a few of which have survived. Architectural members from churches of the Byzantine period and the period of the Knights were used in the construction of it. The **Mosque of Sultan Mustafa** lies in a small square in a side street to the E. of Ippodamou street. It was built in 1765, and there is a Turkish *Hamam* (Bath) in the same square, that was contemporary with it. The small **Mosque of Aga** in Sokratous street is a more recent, lighter building. Another point of interest in the old town is the **Library of Ahmet Havuz,** which contains many Turkish, Arabic and Persian manuscripts, including an illustrated Koran of 1540 and a chronicle of the siege of 1522. It was built by a Rhodian moslem Aga. The clock Tower NE of the Mosque of Suleiman was built in the 19th century.

In the N. part of the new town, near the Government House, there is another interesting **mosque** which took its name from the Suleiman's admiral **Murat Reis,** who was killed during the siege of 1522 and is buried there. Turkish officials and other Moslems of different nationalities who had lived in exile on the island are buried in the cemetery around him; among them are a Persian Shah, Grand Viziers and Pashas, and also an exiled 18th-century poet, Mohammed Ahmet.

The Modern City

The growth of the city outside the walls was the result of the expulsion of the Greek population from the old town in 1522. Most of the building activity has taken place during the last fifty years, however, and is due to the mania of the Italian conquerors for building, and to the development of tourism during the last 20 years. The rather bulky Italian buildings lend a curious character to Mandraki, which resembles a film set of a city just abandoned by its inhabitants. These buildings were constructed in a mixture of styles in which Venetian, Gothic and Arabic elements exist side by side, and they include the New Market Place, the Law Courts, the Post Office, the Church of St John-the Annunciation, the Government House, the Port

Authority building and others. The Aquarium, at the N. extremity of the city, is worth visiting, since it is the only museum of its kind in Greece.

LINDOS

The acropolis of Lindos, which towers above the open sea, is one of the places that have aroused men's admiration since ancient times. Its beauty derives from a combination of the natural setting and the works of man that stand on the rock, 116 m. above the waters. Lindos first became important in the prehistoric period, as is shown by the worship of Athena Lindia. An inscription discovered at Lindos and now in the Copenhagen Museum, known as the *"Lindian Chronicle"*, may give some idea of the importance and prosperity of the sanctuary from as early as the prehistoric period. The inscription was the work of the Lindian writer Timachidas, and was incised in 99 B.C.; amongst other things, it includes a list of gifts dedicated from time to time in the temple by various rulers and other donors. An important pointer to the renown of the ancient past of the sanctuary is to be found in the fact that the first 14 donors mentioned in the list are mythical figures, such as the Telchines, Kadmos, Minos, Herakles, Helen and so on.

Lindos shared in the first period of Rhodes' prosperity along with the other two Dorian city-states on the island, and played a leading role in founding colonies, in commerce and in seafaring. In the first half of the 6th century B.C., it was ruled for 40 years by Kleoboulos, one of the Seven Sages. A larger temple to the goddess was constructed during his rule, replacing the earlier one dating from the Geometric period. The temple burned down in 342 B.C. but was later rebuilt to the same plan. Although Lindos lost its political importance after the synoecism of 408 B.C., the economic life and the fame of the sanctuary do not appear to have been adversely affected by it. This is apparent from the works executed on the acropolis shortly after that date, not least the propylaia. The grandiose buildings which gave the acropolis its final form were erected in Hellenistic times. Lindos was continuously inhabited throughout history. In the Byzantine period the acropolis was fortified first by the Byzantines and then by the Knights, and during the period of the Knights the fortresses of Lindos, Faraklos and Filerimos were the strongest outside Rhodes.

Lindos was excavated by Danish archaeologists during the present century (1902-1914); restoration work on the buildings on the acropolis was undertaken by the Italians.

To visit the acropolis today, one passes through the medieval wall, ascends the staircase to the palace of the Commander of the Castle under the Knights, and then comes to the area of the ancient sanctuary. On the terrace on which one stands before ascending the staircase to the acropolis, there is an *exedra* carved out of the rock on the left, part of the Byzantine fortification, and a relief depicting the **stern of a Hellenistic ship.** The boat served as a base for the statue of the admiral Hagesandros, as an inscription tells us, and was the work of the sculptor Pythokritos (beginning of the 2nd century B.C.), who is thought to have been the creator of the famous Victory of

Samothrace. As one ascends the rather steep staircase to the entrance to the Castle, which was built in the period of the Grand Master Fluvian (1421-1437) or d'Aubusson (1476-1503) – their coats of arms may be seen on a window of the Commandery – one can see some remains of the ancient staircase on the left. The entrance to the acropolis in ancient times must have been at the same point on the N. side of the rock. Next to the medieval Commandery are the remains of the Byzantine **church of St John** (13th century). As one proceeds to the E. and approaches the sanctuary, one passes through the medieval building and comes out opposite a staircase that leads to an area rather like a large square. A series of vaults to the right and left of the staircase support this artificial square or terrace. The staircase and the vaulting date from the 1st century B.C. In the area to the N. of the staircase, there are a large number of bases from dedications; an *exedra*

19. Reconstruction of the acropolis at Lindos in the Hellenistic Period according to E. Dyggve. The reconstruction of the Roman temple to the fore is completely imaginary.

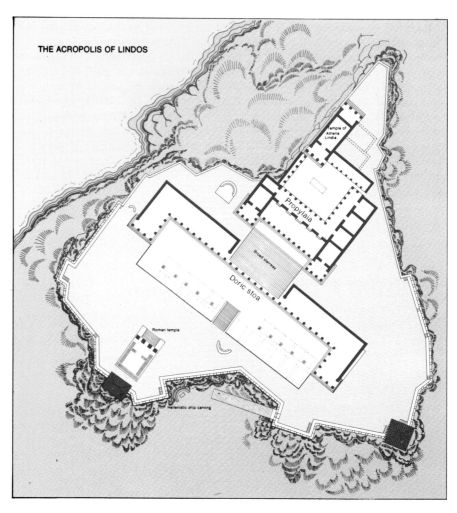

THE ACROPOLIS OF LINDOS

Temple of Athena Lindia

Propylaia

Broad staircase

Doric stoa

Roman temple

Hellenistic ship carving

20. Plan of the Hellenistic sanctuary of Athena on the acropolis of Lindos.

from the end of the 3rd century B.C., on which stood the statue of a man named Pamphilidas, according to the inscription on it; the foundations of a small temple dating from the Roman period, etc.

By way of the staircase one approaches the large **Doric stoa** that stands before the propylaia, and gives a certain majesty to the approach to the temple. It was a double-winged stoa orientated to the N. facing the temple. Built about 200 B.C., it has on overall length of 88 m. and is 9 m. wide; it had a total of 42 columns, of which 20 are now standing. The 8 central columns of the façade stand in front of the marvellous monumental staircase that leads to the propylaia, and there was no wall behind them, because this would have blocked the view of the staircase. The latter has 34 steps and is 21 m. wide; it was built after 408 B.C., during the 4th century, as was the propylaia which was modelled on that of the Athenian Acropolis. Only its foundations survive. The **propylaia** consisted of an outer row of columns to the north, forming three sides of a large rectangle with the same orientation as the double-winged stoa, and a row to the south in the shape of an L, whose open side faced the temple. There were rooms between the colonnades, more of them on the west side than on the east, since the temple was virtually opposite the east side. The **Temple of Athena Lindia,** oriented NE-SW, is a Doric amphiprostyle temple (that is, it only has columns on the shorter sides), with four columns. It is in quite a good state of preservation (first half of the 4th century B.C.). The statue of Athena in the 4th-century temple depicted the goddess standing with her shield in her left hand, and was gold and ivory like its model on the Athenian Acropolis. From the southern edge of the acropolis one can see the small harbour of St Paul.

Monuments Outside the Acropolis

The **theatre** of the ancient city is on the western slope of the acropolis; it has 26 rows of seats and dates from the 4th century B.C. On the northern slope there is a small shrine of the Geometric period (10th-9th century B.C.), called the **"Boukopion",** in which bulls were sacrificed. According to myth, the sacrifices offered to the goddess Lindia were bloodless, and this is thought to be the reason why the animal sacrifices took place here, outside the sanctuary. Despite the evidence of the myths, however, animals were in fact sacrificed within the sanctuary of the goddess.

The area around Lindos is full of ancient cemeteries. It is worth mentioning a large Hellenistic tomb at the end of the promontory that protects the large harbour to the north. Known, erroneously, as the **tomb of Kleoboulos,** it is circular, 9 m. in diameter, and encloses a rectangular burial chamber. It was converted into a Christian church of St Aimilianos.

The village at the foot of the acropolis extends to the N. and the W. and lies on the site of the ancient city. The site appears to have been abandoned between the 6th and 10th centuries A.D., when the inhabitants went to live on the acropolis or on their farms. It would appear from the churches that began to be built in the 11th century, that the village was re-inhabited from that date, and later knew times of great fortune. The prosperity of the inhabitants in the 15th and 16th centuries is clear from the large houses constructed then. Their wealth derived from seafaring. Many of the 17th-century houses in the village are still preserved, and the oldest house is inscribed with the date 1599. The main architectural features of these houses are the high wall facing the road and the apsidal entrance leading into the courtyard; inside the yard the house consists mainly of one large room, with a large vault in the centre to support the roof. Many of the houses have façades with ornamentation incised in the stone, usually around the door and windows; the motifs include rosettes, birds etc. The Lindian pottery, mainly plates, that adorns the interior of many houses, was first made in the 16th century A.D. According to tradition, the Knights captured a boat carrying Persian craftsmen and held them on Rhodes, where they taught the art of pottery. The Lindian plates certainly show eastern influence. They reached their height in the 16th and 17th centuries; they have polychrome decoration, with motifs that mainly depict vegetation, and more rarely animals or human figures. A large number of them are on exhibition in the Benaki Museum in Athens.

In the village there is the large octagonal-domed, cruciform **church of the Virgin** (Panaghia); it has an inscription with the date 1489/90, and the coat of arms of the Grand Master d'Aubusson, though it is not certain that it was built then. Perhaps the W. narthex was added at that date. At one time it was the *katholikon* of a monastery, nowadays it is a parish church. The wall-paintings, were executed in 1799 by Gregorios of Syme, as mentioned in the inscription over the N. door. There is a fine wood-carved iconostasis.

IALYSOS

Archaeological research has demonstrated that the area around ancient Ialysos was inhabited from the Minoan and Mycenaean periods. The city lay 10 kms to the west of Rhodes, around and above Mt Filerimos. In the historical period the acropolis of Ialysos was called Achaea, a name surviving from the Mycenaean period. The earliest settlement in the area, Minoan Ialysos, was on the western edge of the modern village of that name. The Mycenaean cemeteries were at the sites of Moskou Vounara and Makria Vounara, on the foothills of Filerimos, while those of the Geometric and Archaic periods lay between the villages of Kremasti and Trianda. The large area they covered has led some scholars to suggest that the city was not concentrated in one spot, but consisted of a number of rural demes. The finds from the excavations are in the Rhodes Archaeological Museum.

The upper part of Filerimos is a large plateau, and most of the buildings from the periods during which Filerimos was occupied are on the eastern side of it. They include the foundations of the **temple of Athena Polias.** This was a Doric temple and would have been similar in form to that of Athena Lindia – that is it was amphiprostyle – but was bigger and had 6 columns in front and back. It dates from the 3rd or 2nd century B.C., but here too, as at Lindos, there will have been an earlier temple, for the worship of Athena is attested from the 9th century B.C. onwards. The clay antefixes with representations of gorgoneia, found here, probably come from an earlier temple, perhaps built after the Persian Wars. There is an Early Christian **basilica** on top of most of the Hellenistic temple; it dates from the 5th or 6th century A.D. and appears to have been the reason for the ultimate destruction of the temple. The east part of the church is preserved; a cross-shaped font of the baptistery may be been in the S. apse of the sanctuary. There are architectural members from the basilica in the Rhodes Archaeological Museum.

The other monuments in the area furnish evidence for the later history of the site. In 1248 the Genoese besieged John Cantacuzenus here; in 1306, the Knights seized the castle before they captured Rhodes; and it was here that Suleiman established his headquarters in 1522. The Byzantine fortifications may be seen on the E. edge and at the NW corner of the hill. Ancient material, including columns from the temple of Athena, was used in their construction.

The Knights extended the fortifications and built a monastery and a church on the site of the earlier Byzantine church. The monastery that one sees today, with a courtyard surrounded by cloisters and cells, was rebuilt by the

Italians. In the same area may still be seen the small subterranean Byzantine church of **Aghios Georgios o Chostos**, which has frescoes showing Western influence (14th and 15th centuries), and also the remains of the *katholikon* and a number of cells of the Byzantine monastery (10th century).

A road called **Calvary** (Golgothas), which has scenes of the Passion on both sides of it, leads to the western part of the hill. There is a panoramic view from the end of it, dominated by Mt Atavyros in the distance. Thirty metres below the S. side of the hill there is a well-preserved and partly restored **fountain** with 6 Doric columns and 6 stone piers inside it. Behind these was the reservoir and between them a parapet with lion heads (4th century B.C.).

KAMIROS

Kamiros, on the NW coast of the island, seems from the myths and the archaeological evidence to have been inhabited from the prehistoric period. The myth of Althaimenes reflects the establishment of the Minoans in the area, and excavation has demonstrated that Kamiros flourished before the Dorian colonisation. Mycenaean cemeteries have been located at Kalavarda, to the E. of Kamiros.

Nearly all the hills around the ancient city are full of ancient cemeteries. One of them is Fikellura, from which the Rhodian vases of this type derive their name. The funerary stele of Krito and Timarista, one of the choicest exhibits in the Rhodes Archaeological Museum, was recovered from another cemetery hereabouts. Kamiros reached the peak of its prosperity at the same time as the other two Dorian cities, and began to decline after the synoecism of 408 B.C. It was the smallest of the three Dorian cities, and continued to be inhabited until the early centuries of the Christian era, when at some point in time it was abandoned. A visit to the excavated area of the city gives one the opportunity of seeing not only the sanctuaries and public buildings that can usually be seen at other archaeological sites, but also the houses and roads of a Hellenistic city. The city developed in a valley. The **acropolis,** which was unfortified as was the city itself, was on the highest point to the south. The N. part of the city is built in the shape of an amphitheatre facing the sea, and was the area of the public buildings. The acropolis is 120 m. above sea-level. Here stood the **temple of Athena Camirus**, which may have been peripteral. In places, the foundations of the perimeter wall of the sanctuary and of the temple (3rd-2nd century B.C.) can be seen. On the N. part of the hill that formed the acropolis there is a large fountain (6th or 5th century B.C.), which has a capacity of 600 cubic metres. Later, at the end of the 3rd century B.C., a large **stoa,** with an E-W orientation, was built in front of the N. side of the hill. It was 200 m. long and had two rows of Doric columns. The rooms behind the rows of columns were probably for overnight stays by worshippers at the temple. The reservoir fell into disuse with the reconstruction of the Stoa and was replaced by wells and a subterranean system that collected and distributed the water.

The area of the city occupied by private houses, which has been excavated, spreads out to the north of the acropolis; it represents only part of its total extent. Some of the houses are quite well preserved and have an interior courtyard surrounded by a colonnade.

The N. side of the city, in which many of the public buildings were centred, acquired its final form in the Hellenistic period (3rd-2nd century B.C.). In the W. section of this area there was a **temple,** dedicated in all probability to **Pythian Apollo,** of which the foundations may be seen. The inscribed bases show clearly that there were a large number of dedications near the temple; they include an Ionic *naiskos*. There is a large **fountain** to the SE of the temple. In the NE section of the platform there is an enclosure containing altars at two levels, dedicated to the gods; one of them was a dedication to Helios. The two *kouroi* in the Rhodes Archaeological Museum were discovered here.

OTHER PLACES OF INTEREST ON THE ISLAND

The places so far described do not exhaust the interest of Rhodes. A tour of the island reveals a whole series of points of interest, as well as affording opportunities to enjoy its natural beauty. Most of the villages on Rhodes have been continuously inhabited from the Byzantine period or the period of the Knights, as is clear either from the existence in some of them of Byzantine churches, or references to them in documents dating from the period of the Knights. Some villages had a fortress on a high point and spread out around the foot of it. A fine example of this is **Archangelos** (33 kms S. of Rhodes), the traditional part of which is preserved intact, despite all the new concrete buildings in the lower part of it. The Knights' castle on the peak of the hill has the coat of arms of the Grand Master Orsini. The village has a church of St John the Baptist (Aghios Ioannis o Prodromos) with very badly preserved 14th-century frescoes, and also a 19th-century church of the Taxiarchs, whose tall campanile is visible far and wide. Outside the village is the church of Sts Theodore (Aghioi Theodoroi), with frescoes dated by an inscription to 1372.

One of the finest spots on the island is the **castle of Monolithos** (89 kms S. of Rhodes and 2 kms SW of the village of that name); one can see it either from above, if one approaches it by the road, which is higher than the castle, or by climbing up to it on foot.

In addition to Lindos and Archangelos, **Asklepeio** is another village worth visiting; it has a fine layout and domestic architecture, a castle and a Byzantine church of the Dormition of the Virgin; this is in the shape of a cross and has some very interesting frescoes, which have been unjustly described by some scholars as badly executed.

Other villages of interest are **Koskinou,** which has some fine houses with decorated doors to their courtyards, and **Embona** (60 kms from Rhodes), where the traditional costume and embroidery are preserved alongside the traditional village plan. It is possible from Embona, with the aid of a guide, to ascend to the peak of Atavyros, on which was the sanctuary of Zeus.

Ths island has a considerable number of remote churches and monasteries that are of some interest (Aghios Nikolaos Foundoukli, Taxiarchs at Thari).

21. Plan of ancient Kamiros. The city extends over a valley and the main street follows its axis with the city blocks to left and right. A large portico formed the northern boundary of the city of Kamiros.

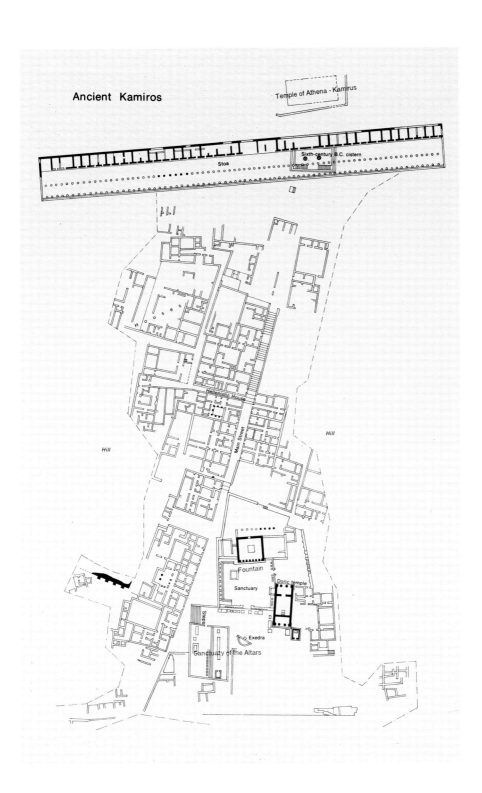

Ancient Kamiros

Temple of Athena - Kamirus

Stoa

Sixth-century B.C. cistern

Hill

HOUSES

Hellenistic House

Main Street

Hill

Fountain

Sanctuary

Doric temple

Steps

Exedra

Sanctuary of the Altars

◀ *22. General view of the harbour of Rhodes.*

23. View of Mandraki, the smaller of the two harbours of Rhodes; small vessels moor here.

24. The New Market and Mandraki, from the Palace of the Grand Master. The New Market is a large polygonal building with arcades on the exterior and a large open space inside that serves as a market.

23

25-27. Three views of Rhodes by night: the Palace of the Grand Master, the Government House and Mandraki.

28

28. *View of the Government House, a modern building with Gothic and Renaissance architectural features.*

29. *The church of the Annunciation, built on the plan of the earlier Gothic church of Saint John from the period of the Knights.*

30. The entrance to Mandraki with the famous bronze hind, one of the most distinctive features of modern Rhodes.

31. The three windmills on the mole of Saint Nicholas.

31

32. *The small, restored theatre on the acropolis of Rhodes.*

33. *The stadium has also been restored, almost in its entirety.*

34. *Very few monuments have survived from the acropolis of ancient Rhodes. One of the most important of them is the temple of Pythian Apollo pictured here.*

34

35. *The Palace of the Grand Master had a dual function; it was at once the residence of the Grand Master of the Order of Saint John and part of the defensive system. Very few parts of the original medieval building survive. Most of it was restored by the Italian governor De Vecchi.*

36. *The entrance of the Palace of the Grand Master. It is flanked by semi-circular towers surmounted by battlements.*

37. *The large inner courtyard of the Palace of the Grand Master. The Knights stored ammunition and food below it, to be used in the event of siege.*

7

38. The large colonnaded hall in the Palace of the Grand Master. The councils of the Order of Saint John may have been held here.

39. The great staircase of the Palace of the Grand Master.

38

40. *Argyrokastrou square, with the old hospital of the Knights, which was built in the 14th century and now houses the offices of the Archaeological Service and the Archaeological Library. In the middle of the square there is an Early Christian font which has been converted into a fountain.*

41. *The Street of the Knights, with the "Inns" of the "Tongues" right and left, was the main street in the Collachium. It is one of the best preserved medieval streets in Europe, and has a striking atmosphere.*

40

42. *The Saint John Gate.*

43. *The Sea Gate near the commercial harbour. The entrance stands between two imposing towers. The emblem of P. d'Aubusson and a relief portraying the Virgin Mary between Saint Peter and Saint Paul can be seen above the entrance.*

42

44. The fortification walls on the side of the commercial harbour.

45. Aghiou Fanouriou street, one of the oldest streets in the Burgum.

44

46. Ippokratous square with its fountain.

47. The square of the Jewish Martyrs, with the Archbishopric on the left (erroneously known as the Admiralty). In the centre is the fountain with seahorses.

◀ *48. General view of the acropolis, the village and the harbour of Lindos.*

49. The architecture of the houses at Lindos is a mixture of Gothic, Byzantine and Islamic elements deriving from the different cultures that have set their seal on the village. The façades were adorned with decorative reliefs and inscriptions.

50. The rooftops of Lindos.

50

51. The exedra and the ship carved in relief on the rock outside the acropolis at Lindos. The ship was used as the base for the statue of Hagesandros.

52. The medieval entrance to the acropolis at Lindos. On the left is the palace of the commander of the fortress in the period of the Knights.

◀ *53. General view of the large Doric stoa. The ends turn in at right angles. On the left is the temple of Athena.*

54. The eastern part of the Doric stoa on the acropolis at Lindos.

55. The temple of Athena was Doric and had four columns at the ends. It was built in the first half of the 4th century B.C.

56. The sheer cliff at Lindos rises vertically to a height of 116 m. above the sea. Above and around it Lindos "rejoices in the ocean", as an ancient epigram says.

57. View of the Hellenistic remains of Kamiros with the sea in the back-ground. The city was built in a valley, a short distance from the shore.

58. The area of the sanctuary in the lower part of the city.

8

59. *The residential quarter of Kamiros. The restored columns belong to the peristyle of a private house.*

60. *The main street of the city started from the Doric temple and ran along the valley. The steps that can be seen in the photograph led to the upper part of the city.*

60

61. *View of the restored monastery at Filerimos, founded by the Knights of Saint John.*

62. *The road to the monastery at Filerimos.*

61

63. *The south façade of the church of the Virgin (Panaghia) at Filerimos, a restored Gothic church built on the site of the ancient city of Ialysos. There is the baptistery of an Early Christian basilica within the fenced area.*

64. *The Byzantine church of Aghios Nikolaos (Foundoukli) on Profitis Ilias.*

65. *The hot springs at Kallithea.*

66. *The valley of the butterflies. The butterflies do not always make their appearance, but the valley is cool and verdant.*

66

THE MUSEUMS OF RHODES

Archaeological Museum

This is housed in the Hospital of the Knights. A visit to it is interesting not only for the exhibits, which range in chronological terms from the Mycenaean period to the Early Christian, and also include a number of reliefs from the period of the Knights, but also for the building itself. The lower floor is not open to the public.

The *Central Courtyard* houses a Hellenistic lion and large numbers of stone and iron cannon balls from the various sieges of the city.

The exhibits on the *upper floor* are housed in rooms that look onto the arcade and the central courtyard. The arcade contains a large number of small reliefs, altars, inscriptions (including an Archaic one dating from the 6th century B.C.), a sarcophagus of the Klazomenai style from Ialysos, etc. The rooms on the S. side contain finds from the excavations of the cemeteries in the area of ancient Ialysos; they are displayed by tomb and consist mainly of vases dating from the 9th to the 5th century B.C. The Corinthian vases and a number of Egyptian objects in the first room are of particular interest, as are the Attic black- and red-figure vases in the third. The first room on the W. side contains Rhodian pottery from the Protogeometric and Geometric periods, Attic black-figure ware, and a Rhodian amphora of the Fikellura type. A Lakonian *hydria* has a representation of a duel, with the names of the combatants. The next room has a series of fine Attic vases, including a particularly distinctive one depicting Dionysos and satyrs. Equally interesting are the clay masks and the terracotta idols depicting a dead man in his bed and a seated woman bewailing him, made from a separate piece. The following rooms on this side are temporarily closed. They contain Mycenaean grave goods from the area of Ialysos, including some jewellery; objects from the excavations at Kamiros; Rhodian coins; white lekythoi; and gold jewellery from the Classical period. The rooms on the N. side house finds from Kamiros. The first room beyond the NW corner, and the staircase which leads out of the Museum into the street of the Knights, contains Protogeometric and Geometric vases from the excavations at Kamiros. In the next room there are 7th-century B.C. vases, dominated by the Rhodian *oinochoe* with bands of decoration depicting animals or plant motifs. The following rooms contain Rhodian plates from the same period, depicting sphinxes, Rhodian vases, of the Fikellura style, and so on.

In the middle of the E. side is the entrance to the *great sick ward,* which is divided into two aisles by a row of pointed arches. There is a side chapel opposite the entrance. The ward itself contains relief grave stones from the period of the Knights, and a large number of coats of arms.

In the large room in the south part of the ward, which was once the refectory or dining room for the hospital staff, there is a display of funerary *stelai* from the Roman period. The following room is dominated by the stele of Krito and Timarista; two female figures, the dead mother, Timarista (on the right), and her daughter, Krito, are embracing in a final farewell (end of the 5th century B.C.). This room also contains other Classical funerary *stelai*, one of which potrays the deceased with his young servant. Next to the stele of Krito is a seated female figure, of which the upper part is preserved (5th century B.C.). A relief in the Severe Style (460 B.C.) depicting a boy, and the fine stele of Kalliarista (4th century B.C.), catch the attention here, as does the head and part of the body of a female figure from a Hellenistic funerary monument. A grave stele (2nd century B.C.) from the city cemetery of the Hellenistic period depicts a hoplite holding his helmet in his hand.

The room containing Archaic works is adorned with two marble *kouroi* from Kamiros. One of them was made in a Naxian workshop (550-525 B.C.). The fragment of a *kouros'* head on the walls is of interest for the way in which the hair is worked.

The room of the large Aphrodite contains the statue of the godess "Aidoumene" ("Pudica"); it is considerably corroded, for it was found in the sea. Other works in this room are: the fine headless statue of a Nymph with her foot on a rock (1st century B.C.); the head of the god Helios with holes around the hair to hold metal rays (first half of the 2nd century B.C.); the head of an athlete (2nd century B.C.), and a head that possibly portrays the philosopher Apollonios (1st century B.C.). The "Hekataion" with three female figures was discovered on the acropolis of Rhodes.

In the *corridor* next to this room there is displayed a fine head of the god Bacchus, made of porphyry, which was discovered in the village of Soroni (2nd or 1st century B.C.).

The room of the small Aphrodite contains the most famous work in the Museum. Aphrodite is represented kneeling, either before or after her bath, in a posture that indicates that she is either loosening or tying up her hair. It is a reworking of a famous earlier work by the sculptor Doidalsas (1st century B.C.). In this room there is also a series of small statues, the most distinctive of which is that of Asklepios with the snake twined around his staff. The headless statue of a Nymph sitting on a rock (1st century B.C.); a variety of other seated or standing figures; a satyr stretched out on a wineskin (2nd century B.C.); and a fine intoxicated Dionysos (2nd century B.C.) are amongst the other works displayed in this room.

The small room of Menander is dominated by the portrait of the comic poet; it is a copy of the statue of him made in the workshop of the sons of Praxiteles. Opposite, there are two fine Roman heads, one of them badly broken.

The Museum Garden contains a variety of architectural members, altars, grave *stelai* and funerary monuments, including one in the form of a small temple with a Roman statue in it. The dolphin, made of dark stone, with the young dolphin beside it, is particularly charming.

Art Gallery

The last few years have seen the creation in Rhodes of a very important art gallery, containing mainly works by 20th-century Greek painters. It is housed on the upper floor of the Ionic Bank building in the old city. It possesses over 300 paintings, representative of a large number of contemporary painters. Amongst those in the first room (A) are works by: Parthenis, Bouzianis and Argyros, and some of the few sculptures belonging to the collection by Apartis, Zongolopoulos and Lameras.

Amongst the painting in Room Δ are five by Theophilos: the brigand Davelis, the meeting of Erotokritos and Aretousa, Pavlos Melas etc. Works by Kondoglou and Sikeliotis are exhibited along with them. Room Γ has paintings by Engonopoulos, Tsarouchis, Spyropoulos, Chatzikyriakos-Gikas, Mavroidis, Gaïtis, Tetsis, and many other well-known artists.

Folk Art Collection

The Folk Art Collection is a charming little museum which is housed in the Arsenal of the Knights, in Argyrokastrou square. There is a tasteful exhibition of furniture, costumes, pottery and other vessels, representing the folk art of the island and the rest of the Dodecanese during the last few centuries. The *sperveri* deserves particular attention; this was an embroidered curtain that was hung in front of the bridal bed. The exhibits in the collection make a distinct contribution to the picture of how life was lived a few years ago, that one forms from visiting the villages.

67. The entrance to the hospital of the Knights, a striking Gothic building dating from the 15th century (building commenced in 1440). It now houses the Archaeological Museum of Rhodes.

68

69

68. *Mycenaean vase from Ialysos.*

69-70. *Two vases of the "Fikellura" style (the name derives from a site near Kamiros). The decoration of these vases makes use of subjects of the Orientalising style (animals-birds), as well as geometric motifs. 6th century B.C.*

70

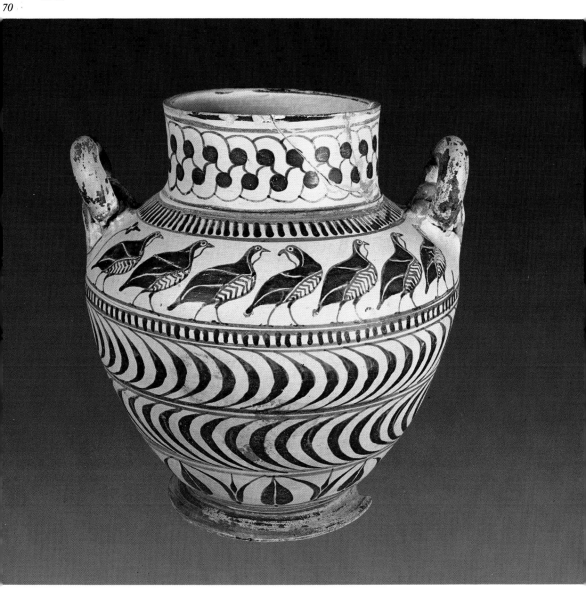

71-72. Two plastic vases in the shape of human heads. First half of the 5th century B.C.

73. Rhodian oinochoe, with trefoil mouth decorated with animals. 7th century B.C.

71

72

73

74. *Torso of a kouros from Kamiros. From an island workshop (Paros?). Second half of the 6th century B.C.*

75. *Terracotta female protome with traces of colour. First half of the 5th century B.C.*

76. *The grave stele of Krito and Timarista. The girl, Krito, is embracing her mother in a final farewell. Her hair is cut short as a sign of mourning. The delicate workmanship indicates that it was produced by an Ionian workshop. An outstanding work from the end of the 5th century B.C.*

77. *Female head with delicate sensitive features and a sad expression. Detail from a funerary statue dating from the second half of the 4th century B.C.*

78. *Grave stele of a dead warrior. 2nd century B.C.* ▶

79. *Grave stele depicting the dead woman, seated, and a slave girl. First half of the 4th century B.C.* ▶

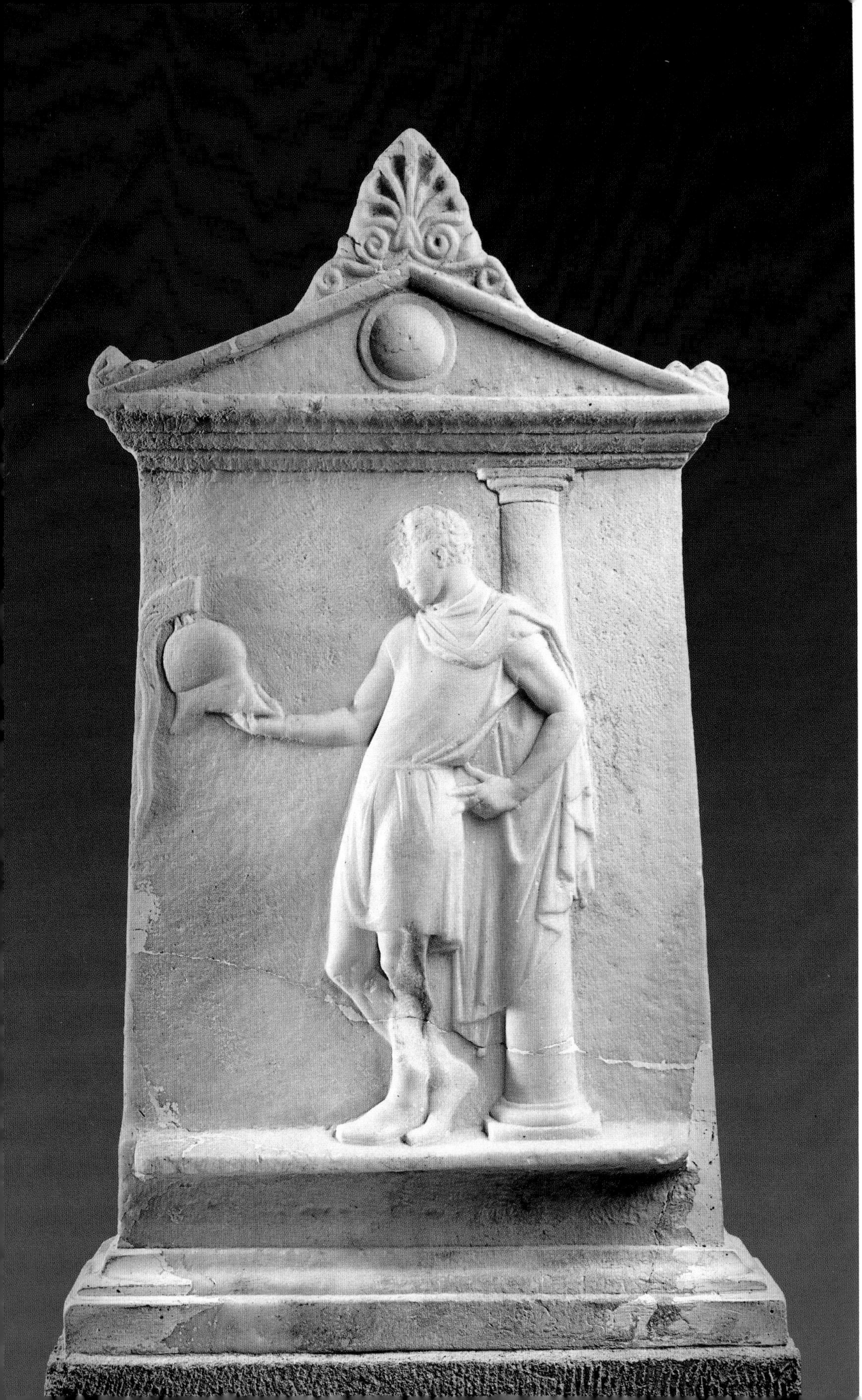

78

80. *Roman statuette of the god Asklepios.*

81. Roman statuette of the goddess Hygeia.

82. *Statue of Dionysos. A typical piece of Hellenistic baroque. 2nd century B.C.*

83. *Head of Helios, perhaps from a pediment. A good example of Hellenistic baroque. The holes in the hair were sockets into which the metal rays were fitted. 2nd century B.C.*

84. *Head of an athlete. Outstanding work of art from the 2nd century B.C.*

85. *Aphrodite bathing, a copy of a work by the Bithynian artist Doidalsas. The goddess is resting on one knee and drying her hair. 1st century B.C.*

 87

-87. *Two statues of
mphs. The contrast
tween the surface of
bodies and the folds
the clothes is cleverly
ntrived. First half of
e 1st century B.C.*

88. *The Muse Thaleia. Detail from a mosaic floor depicting the Nine Muses. 1st century A.D.*

89. *Mosaic depicting a theatrical mask. Rhodes, Archaeological Museum.*

90. *Hellenistic and Roman mosaics from Kos and other islands in the Dodecanese are housed in the Palace of the Grand Master. The most famous is the scene of a lion hunt from a mosaic floor dating from Roman times.*

91. *Lindian jug dating from the 16th century, with a scene of heraldic goats. Lindian pottery dates from the 16th century and afterwards. It is not clear whether it was made on Rhodes or at Nikaia in Asia Minor. Athens, Benaki Museum.*

92. *Rhodian plate with a scene of a three-masted schooner. Athens, Benaki Museum.*

93. *Plate, of the kind made for use in churches, decorated with a lion and oriental flowers. The Greek inscription on the border reads: "Sun of justice, Christ of our thoughts, our God. 25th May 1666". Athens, Benaki Museum.*

92

93

125

94-95. Rhodian plate, with plant motifs perfectly adapted to the circular shape.

96. Polychrome jug. Rhodes Folk Art Collection.

96

97. *A Rhodian multicoloured sperveri, a kind of heavy curtain embroidered in silk which hung above the bed.*

ΣΠΕΡΒΕΡΙ ΡΟΔΟΥ
17ᵒ-18ᵒ ΑΙΩΝΟΣ